One-Minute
Prayers™
for Men

Text by Hope Lyda

HARVEST HOUSE PUBLISHERS

EUGENE, OREGON

Cover by Garborg Design Works, Savage, Minnesota

Cover photo © Oliver Childs / iStockphoto

ONE-MINUTE PRAYERS™ FOR MEN GIFT EDITION
Copyright © 2004/2010 by Harvest House Publishers
Eugene, Oregon 97402
www.harvesthousepublishers.com

ISBN 978-0-7369-2821-2

Printed in China

11 12 13 14 15 16 17 / RDS-SK / 10 9 8 7 6 5

Contents

Give.	5
Receive	6
Abilities	9
Provision	15
Identity	21
Asking for Directions.	27
Cooperation	33
Silence.	39
Communication	45
Learning to Be.	51
Trust	57
Real Manhood.	63
Vocation	69
Freedom	75
Fatherhood	81
Integrity	87
Success	93
True Strength.	99
Management	105
Leading.	111
Marriage	117
Connection	123
Worry	129
Power	135

Covenant.   141
Friendship.   147
Serving   153
Vision   159
Eternity.   165
Sexuality   171
Health   177
Work.   183
Temptation   189
Choices   195
Time   201
Prosperity   207
Hard Times   213
Grace.   219
Praise.   225
The Holy Spirit   231
Thoughts.   237
Love   243
Forgiveness   249
The Poor   255
Pride   261
Helping Others   267
The Words of My Mouth.   273
Confidence   279
Desires.   285

Because His Love Endures Forever

Give thanks to the Lord, for he is good. His love endures forever. Give thanks to the God of gods. His love endures forever. Give thanks to the Lord of lords: His love endures forever.

—PSALM 136:1-3

✍

Lord, thank You for the life You have given me. Upon rising in the morning, I worship the Lord of lords, the God of all gods, and the King of kings...and You call me by name. I think back to the day I met You and how You welcomed me with open arms. You received this prodigal son without hesitation.

For all these reasons and so many more, I give You thanks. I offer up my life to You and Your service. I can think of no greater way to live than to consider each day a holy, living sacrifice to You. May Your will be done through the course of my days.

Receiving Your Promises

So do not throw away your confidence; it will be richly rewarded. You need to persevere so that when you have done the will of God, you will receive what he has promised.

—HEBREWS 10:35-36

✑

You have given me so much, Lord. My offering of thanks and a willing spirit seems so small compared to the expanse of Your mercy. Yet I have confidence that You receive the gift of my days with graciousness...it is Your way. I carry Your love with me through good and bad times; I pay attention to my blessings because they direct me back to the hand of the Giver.

Each day reveals the rewards of a faith lived out. I hunger for a deeper understanding of my purpose under heaven. Give me the courage to do Your will. Open up my heart and my life, Lord, so I can fully receive the promises You have for me.

Abilities

Use It

If a man's gift is prophesying,
let him use it in proportion to his faith.
If it is serving, let him serve; if it is teaching,
let him teach; if it is encouraging,
let him encourage; if it is contributing to the
needs of other people, let him give generously;
if it is leadership, let him govern diligently;
if it is showing mercy, let him do it cheerfully.

—ROMANS 12:6-8

✐

God, thank You for the abilities You have bestowed on me. Along my journey I have faced times of ignoring, neglecting, and abusing my gifts. Forgive me for those times of ignorance. I do not want to disregard Your will in my life. I want to claim it and apply Your truth in all circumstances. I know this will involve using my abilities to serve You and other people.

Show me those gifts I have yet to discover. Show me the way to utilize the abilities I have acknowledged.

Going Beyond Ability

*For I testify that they gave as much as they were
able, and even beyond their ability. Entirely on
their own, they urgently pleaded with us for the
privilege of sharing in this service to the saints.*

—2 CORINTHIANS 8:3-4

∽

Lord, don't let me hold onto my abilities as though
they are mine to govern. When I can serve You by using
the gifts You have given me, do not let me fight the
opportunity because it involves too much time, energy,
or commitment. Most of all, I pray to go beyond earthly
expectations. I pray to move past the limitations set by
human standards. Let me push forth in my work, my
life, my faith, and serve You better.

It is a privilege to serve You and the body of Christ
with my natural strengths. Let me keep this in mind as
I face decisions and possibilities. May I always seek more
ways to serve You, Lord.

Not for Sale

When Simon saw that the Spirit was given at the laying on of the apostles' hands, he offered them money and said, "Give me also this ability so that everyone on whom I lay my hands may receive the Holy Spirit."

—ACTS 8:18-19

❧

God, guide me toward Your great purpose in my life. Use me to serve the needs of other people in Your body and of Your creation. Let me not covet the success of other people because it causes me to want their gifts. When I see the achievements of other people, I begin to question my own status in the world. Lead me to a deeper, more meaningful understanding of Your plan, Lord.

When I am tempted to pursue at any cost a journey that is not meant to be mine, may I encounter the truth of Your Word, the wisdom of Your truth, and the wonder of my own life. I want to experience Your will, Lord, not the trappings of another person's path.

From the Same Source

*There are different kinds of gifts, but the same
Spirit. There are different kinds of service, but the
same Lord. There are different kinds of working,
but the same God works all of them in all men.*

—1 CORINTHIANS 12:4-6

✧

Lord, as I make my way through each day, let me
observe and appreciate the kaleidoscope of talent that is
demonstrated by those I encounter. Humble my spirit
so that I see past my abilities to those of people around
me. May I see Your hand on their lives. May I see Your
will being fulfilled in their actions.

You are the Source of all ability and talent, Lord.
Please let me respect the gifts of other people. It is easy
to focus only on my own journey. Lift my eyes beyond
my private path to see the wonders You are performing
all around me.

Provision

Where Greed Leads

*A stingy man is eager to get rich and is unaware
that poverty awaits him.*

—PROVERBS 28:22

❧

In my quest to provide for myself and my family, Lord,
may I not become greedy and selfish. It is very easy to lust
for things of the world. I can lose sight of the spiritual
priorities You set before me. My goal in life is not to accu-
mulate "stuff" but to seek Your way. I do not want to seek
material success that exceeds Your provision.

I have witnessed the downfall of colleagues and
friends who desired more than they needed, more than
You called them to possess. Everything I have is of You
and from You. Never let my eyes or my hands search to
claim more than what You provide at any given moment
in time. I only want to be rich in spirit, Lord.

Behind Every Great Man

You may say to yourself, "My power and the strength of my hands have produced this wealth for me." But remember the LORD your God, for it is he who gives you the ability to produce wealth, and so confirms his covenant, which he swore to your forefathers, as it is today.

—DEUTERONOMY 8:17-18

❧

There is nothing in my life that does not come from You, Lord. Your blessings from heaven are responsible for my every possession, my every met need, my every reward. When success comes my way and brings provision for myself and other people, I turn to You with a heart of thanksgiving. You are my Source of strength and wealth.

You care for every one of Your children, Lord. I am so thankful to count myself among Your followers. May I use the provision of life and health and opportunity to serve You alone.

His Strength

*If anyone serves, he should do it with the
strength God provides, so that in all things God
may be praised through Jesus Christ.*

—1 PETER 4:11

∽

Lord, You see how my fears keep me from serving
You fully. Let me put aside the insecurities that cripple
me. Let me rely on the strength You provide so that I
come to You every time I have a need. I want to fall at
Your feet every time I face difficulty or conflict. I am
shamed easily, Lord, because of my many inabilities. But
I long to serve You with confidence and might.

Those who know me realize that my strength comes
only from You, Lord. They have seen my weaknesses in
the light of day and realize Your power is responsible
for my every success. May this always be so. And may I
always give You credit each time I show an ounce of
strength, a bit of power, an inkling of understanding.

Fruit of a Good Life

*Our people must learn to devote themselves to
doing what is good, in order that they may provide
for daily necessities and not live unproductive lives.*

—TITUS 3:14

⁂

The choice to do good is presented in so many subtle
ways, Lord. Sometimes it is not even a choice, but an
impulse—a nudge to follow in Your way. During my day,
keep me mindful of the opportunities I have to do the
right thing. May my life be an example to other people.
May my life be seen as productive in Your eyes.

I want to be prayerful throughout my day so I can
tap into Your leading at all times. This guidance is Your
provision. It directs my steps and shepherds me through
life.

Identity

Old Versus New Self

*You were taught, with regard to your former way of
life, to put off your old self, which is being corrupted
by its deceitful desires; to be made new in the attitude
of your minds; and to put on the new self, created to
be like God in true righteousness and holiness.*

—EPHESIANS 4:22-24

❧

God, I am so thankful You love Your creation.
Instead of tossing us away with our collection of frailties,
sins, and ungodly attitudes, You reach down and make
us new beings. Our bruises and blemishes are not
enough to turn Your eyes from us. You do not pass us
up for better possibilities.

I am so humbled when I think of who I was before
I met You. I still have days that reflect the old me, but
now I can come to You with the burden of sin and seek
Your forgiveness. I have experienced Your healing touch,
and my heart has been transformed. May I resemble You
more with each passing day.

Who Am I?

Who am I, O LORD God, and what is my family,
that you have brought me this far? And as if this
were not enough in your sight, O God, you have
spoken about the future of the house of your
servant. You have looked on me as though I were
the most exalted of men, O LORD God.

—1 CHRONICLES 17:16-17

∽

My Christian life experience is a bit like climbing out
of a canyon. The trek has been treacherous at times, and
I have lost my footing, but I have kept my eyes focused
on the summit of Your grace. Too many times I have
been tempted to look down…back at the problems that
tripped my feet, or at the crevices which lodged me in
dark times. But as I climb higher, toward the Source of
all light, I am comforted.

You lead me, Lord. You preserve me and my path.
You have lifted me out of my sinful life. Why is it that
You have brought me so far, Lord? May I reach for the
stronghold of Your wisdom and continue along this way
in gratitude.

Known

O LORD, you have searched me and you know me.
You know when I sit and when I rise; you perceive
my thoughts from afar.

—PSALM 139:1-2

❧

Lord, while I might keep to myself around other people, or limit what I share, I take great comfort in being vulnerable and open with You. You know every detail about me: how I am made, the ways in which I struggle, my deepest joys, and the future I will experience. There is such peace in being truly, completely known.

God, help me take this sense of security and turn it into confidence for my relationships with friends, family, and anyone I encounter. Keep me from putting up a facade to protect my heart or my pride. It is time to share the "real me" more openly with the body of Christ and those who do not know You. I seek Your strength as I work toward this goal.

Child of God

*This is how we know who the children of God are
and who the children of the devil are: Anyone who
does not do what is right is not a child of God; nor
is anyone who does not love his brother.*

—1 JOHN 3:10

❧

Lord, do I love enough? Do I pass along Your goodness to other people? I want to be known as a child of God. Where I am resistant to show love or express Your mercy, open up my heart. If I am quick to judge and slow to help another person, push me into action. I get so caught up trying to be who I am in the world that I forget how to be Your son.

I seek balance where these two identities should merge, Lord. Help me pare away characteristics and sins that do not represent You, my heavenly Father. Let me be Your hands and Your heart wherever I may go.

Asking for Directions

Finally, I Am Asking

Hear my cry, O God; listen to my prayer.

—PSALM 61:1

∽

My struggles lately have led me away from my Source of help: You. At first I thought I could figure out the answers on my own. But as I tried this, I lost my way and started to go deeper inside myself. I didn't even know how to ask people for assistance or advice, so I kept trying to get past my problems and failings. Each wrong turn and dead-end should have brought me back to You. Forgive me, Lord, for refusing to ask for help.

So here I am, finally calling out to You. Help me through this. Hear my cry, Lord. With humility I fall at Your feet and ask for guidance.

Within Your Reach

May your hand be ready to help me, for I have chosen your precepts.

—PSALM 119:173

⁓

I choose Your ways, Lord. When I encounter difficulties, I rely on the guidance of Your precepts. Today I ask You to show me mercy, Lord. Reach down into my current circumstances and redirect my steps so that I stay true to Your will. It is easy to become sidetracked in this busy life. Lead me to ask for help as I need it.

I want to stay faithful to the path You have prepared for me. It is exciting to think about how You are using every day of my life to move me forward and to serve Your purpose.

Asking for Faith

*Immediately the boy's father exclaimed, "I do
believe; help me overcome my unbelief!"*

—MARK 9:24

∽

God, I thank You for allowing me to have doubts
even while I have faith. Your gift of free will also gives
me room to experience a deep belief that becomes
stronger through times of doubt. I ask You to overcome
those moments, days, or even months of unbelief.

Thank You for sending people my way who have
encouraged me to see You during hardship. The gift of
faith is holy and precious. I pray that I will hold onto it
tightly at all times, especially in the midst of doubt.

Pure Motivations

You do not have, because you do not ask God.
When you ask, you do not receive, because you
ask with wrong motives, that you may spend what
you get on your pleasures.

—JAMES 4:2-3

ɔℯ

I have shaken my fists toward heaven, Lord. Forgive
me for being demanding as I ask for things that do not
match Your will. It is out of fear that I insist upon an
answer…no…*the answer* that I want. I feel behind in my
life…in the plans I made for myself. This selfish mode
causes me to lose sight of Your wonderful purpose for
my life.

Tear away from me this spirit of fear and arrogance,
Lord. When I call to You, let my spirit of repentance be
sincere. Let my requests be in line with Your plan. And
when my fears override my understanding of how You
work, quiet my heart so I can hear Your words of
leading.

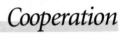

Cooperation

Neighborly Behavior

*Therefore each of you must put off falsehood and
speak truthfully to his neighbor, for we are all
members of one body.*

—EPHESIANS 4:25-26

§

God, rid my language of little white lies—of half-
truths that make the moment easier. Let my exchanges
with strangers and coworkers be as honest as those I
have at home and church. I pray for the wise man's
ability to think before speaking. I have been bound by
less-than-truthful comments or by gossip, and I know
these never end well.

May I never place my pride above truth. May I treat
every person with the respect I have for those closest to
me. Better yet, I will speak to other people in truth as I
do to You.

Called to Peace

Let the peace of Christ rule in your hearts, since
as members of one body you were called to peace.

—COLOSSIANS 3:15

∞

While I try to lead a meaningful and purposeful life, Lord, I know that much of my busyness is caused by insignificant pursuits. I get uptight about little matters and let them fill my heart with anxiety. Release me from these trivial ties to earthly concerns. Pull my thoughts inward and my prayers upward so that I can cooperate with Your Spirit during these times.

I have the eternal Source of peace within me because of Your gift of salvation. May I never take You for granted. Let my success be measured by how well I reflect Your peace to other people in the body of Christ and beyond it.

Seeing Your Work in Others

*In all my prayers for all of you, I always pray with
joy because of your partnership in the gospel from
the first day until now, being confident of this, that
he who began a good work in you will carry it on to
completion until the day of Christ Jesus.*

—PHILIPPIANS 1:4-6

༄

God, my insecurities can rise to the surface when I
face competition in any arena. I put in a lot of time and
am very committed to my job, but this effort should
never distort my view of other people and their worth.

Let me see in all people the good work You have
begun in their hearts. Let that be how I relate to them
at all times...as a fellow child of God, not as a com-
petitor or opponent. Serving You and the church requires
my commitment to kindness and graciousness. Lead me
to encourage other people and look for the good in them
at all times.

Hurdling Sin

*You are still worldly. For since there is jealousy
and quarreling among you, are you not worldly?
Are you not acting like mere men?*

—1 CORINTHIANS 3:3-4

༑

Sin sure can get in the way of a cooperative spirit,
Lord. Sometimes, instead of praying about my sins and
repenting, I hurdle them and try to keep going forward.
Show me how futile this is, Lord. Jealousy and a quick
temper hinder my abilities and also the ways in which
You can work through my life. I become the hurdle to
Your will being accomplished.

As a man, I will sin. As a child of God, I will seek
and find forgiveness so I can stay true to the path of
eternity that is placed before me.

Silence

Silence

A Patient Heart

The LORD is good to those whose hope is in him,
to the one who seeks him; it is good to wait quietly
for the salvation of the LORD.

—LAMENTATIONS 3:25-26

≈

With hope in my heart, I can wait upon Your mercy, Lord. My mouth, so used to forming a string of words, of wants, of grievances, can be closed and still. My voice, so used to crying out, requesting, questioning, can be silenced.

Surrounded by hope, there is no need for the noise of the human mind and heart. Prayers pour forth from my soul. God, thank You for the sanctuary created by the void of words. Encourage me to return to this place more often. When the busy days shout their commands, I will return to Your feet and be thankful for the quiet.

Goodness Silences Ignorance

For it is God's will that by doing good you should
silence the ignorant talk of foolish men.

—1 PETER 2:15

࿐

God, the words spoken in haste by another person seem to have such an impact on me. When a person throws around harsh words in a careless manner, help me see that it is usually ignorance or lack of attention and not evil behind the recklessness.

God, my security is in You. I do not need the validation of other people. Let me turn my concern into prayers for that person's well-being. May I act out a living prayer by responding to strong words with gentle kindness.

Quiet Wisdom

The quiet words of the wise are more to be heeded
than the shouts of a ruler of fools.

—ECCLESIASTES 9:17

❧

Lord, help me stay true to what is right when I am tempted to step out of wisdom and enter the arena of fools. In a meeting the other day I was barely able to voice my opinion while other people freely spoke up, took over, and filled the time for their purposes. Each time I was cut off, my frustration was fueled.

But then You tugged at my heart. I did say what I wanted to express and that was enough. There was no need to compete with their numerous comments and cranked-up volume. You allowed me to remain calm and in control of myself. Thank You for reminding me that You hear every word I speak.

The Hush of Humility

For it is by grace you have been saved, through faith—and this not from yourselves, it is the gift of God—not by works, so that no one can boast.

—EPHESIANS 2:8-9

∽

God, everything I have is from You. The faith I hold onto tightly is a gift of Your grace. If people see the peace and wholeness of my life, may I never claim responsibility for such things. I will share about Your mercy. I will share how Your love transformed me at a time when I could do nothing to help myself.

My dependence on You should shine far brighter than my self-sufficiency. Let everything I do, say, accomplish, or receive praise for be a reflection of Your gift.

Communication

If You Can't Say Anything Nice...

Come, my children, listen to me; I will teach you the fear of the LORD. Whoever of you loves life and desires to see many good days, keep your tongue from evil and your lips from speaking lies.

—PSALM 34:11-13

∽

"Bite your tongue." That is what my mother used to tell me to do when a lie or mean comment was about to slip out of my young mouth. God, You offer me the same advice, and I would be wise to heed it. I believe also that when I am struggling to hold back an unnecessary dig or sarcastic comment, I should look for something good to say at the moment—something righteous and sincere.

Lord, direct my tongue to share the good news. And when that does not surface easily in the heat of the moment, let me fall silent and spend my energy listening for Your direction and awaiting Your peace.

Prayers Translated

We do not know what we ought to pray for, but the Spirit himself intercedes for us with groans that words cannot express.

—ROMANS 8:26

❧

Lord, I fumble along in conversations that have little true significance; therefore, I am so thankful the Spirit intercedes for me when I am at a loss for words. My brokenness cannot be translated into syllables. I can only moan in the midst of darkness. And You are able to decipher every bit of meaning.

The other day, I could not cry or speak. The only sound was that of my heart pounding strongly in my chest. And I knew You understood every beat.

Tell It to Me Straight

Then Jesus' disciples said, "Now you are speaking clearly and without figures of speech. Now we can see that you know all things and that you do not even need to have anyone ask you questions. This makes us believe that you came from God."

—JOHN 16:29-30

❧

Like the disciples who stood by and listened to Your parables and stories and could not fully discern Your truth, I need things spelled out sometimes. I ask You for clear direction in my life right now, Lord. I turn to Your Word for wisdom and am so thankful for its power. I pray that I will be sensitive enough to hear Your messages that are just for me.

In my life, I witness how You guide my steps and lead my heart. My history reveals how personally Your truth impacts my life. The message of Your love becomes very clear…and I know You are God.

Words for Good

*Reckless words pierce like a sword, but the tongue
of the wise brings healing.*

—PROVERBS 12:18

❧

Lord, as I go about my day, let me be watching for
the people who need a healing word. Help me to listen
to the needs being expressed around me. At work, while
business is the topic, encourage my spirit to also listen
to what individuals are saying beneath that conversation.
Is their life difficult right now? Are they excited about a
recent joyful event?

Every conversation I have with another person is
important. The exchange of friendly banter or deep dis-
cussions about faith and life...they all matter because
these dialogues connect me with other beings created in
Your image. Remind me, Lord, to be an encourager.

Learning to Be

How to Live

Make it your ambition to lead a quiet life, to mind your own business and to work with your hands, just as we told you, so that your daily life may win the respect of outsiders and so that you will not be dependent on anybody.

—1 THESSALONIANS 4:11-12

∽

God, You created life to be a process of growing and becoming. Learning how to live becomes a lifelong journey. Just when I think I have arrived at the place where You will surely have me stay, change happens and I am prodded to go further.

As You call me to keep moving and growing, I abide by the guidelines You offer in Your Word. I lead a quiet life focused on You. I mind my own business and strive to earn the respect of other people by working hard. And each day I renew my commitment to walk in Your will.

Resting in the Lord

*On this day, atonement will be made for you, and
you will be cleansed from all your sins in the
LORD's presence. It will be a Sabbath day of total
rest, and you will spend the day in fasting.*

—LEVITICUS 16:30-31 (NLT)

∽

Lord, lead my spirit in the exercise of rest today. I
feel a bit anxious, and my mind keeps visiting all of the
tasks I have to do. But I long to rediscover the practice
of the Sabbath. The world teaches me that I will fall
behind or lose my place if I take time to just "be." But
You call me to take time out for renewal.

May I use my determination to schedule my days to
serve the purpose of the Sabbath. Lead me to be diligent
in this discipline. I pray that I will learn to rest in You.

Every Day
a New Beginning

*In the morning, O LORD, you hear my voice; in the
morning I lay my requests before you and wait in
expectation.*

—PSALM 5:3

∽

I love the morning, Lord. Thank You for allowing
me to experience a beginning every day of my life.
Before my mind turns to the many scheduled items for
the day, I feel the peace of Your presence. When I wake
up early and the light of day is just starting to warm the
earth around me, there is a sense of awe that overcomes
my spirit.

Grant me this feeling of serenity when I am over-
whelmed. When activity replaces a spirit of meditation
and prayer, restore my gratitude from the day's beginning.

Being Myself

*The LORD God formed the man from the dust of
the ground and breathed into his nostrils the
breath of life, and the man became a living being.*

—GENESIS 2:7

∽

Your hand is responsible for forming the physical
shape of mankind. Lord, Your breath entered a form and
turned it into a living being. Help me to embrace this
breath of life…this living spirit that resides within me.
You created wonderful, active beings as Your children.

You could have insisted that we look the same, act
the same, and follow one path…but You didn't. Instead,
You formed each of us as an individual. You breathed
life into our lungs and souls, and we became our unique
selves. Lord, thank You for letting me be myself.

Trust

Share the Load

Trust in him at all times, O people; pour out your hearts to him, for God is our refuge.

—PSALM 62:8

~

I give You the concerns of my heart today, Lord. You know the burdens I am carrying right now. They weigh on my mind and turn my waking moments into chances to worry. I believe You are my Refuge. I do. I just have not allowed You to play that role when it comes to this particular worry. Why do I hold back so much?

I want to trust You with everything in my life. Help me lighten my grip on matters of insignificance. And in matters of great importance and spiritual weight, let me be free to turn them over to You, my Provider, my Lord, my Rock.

God-Reliance

Indeed, in our hearts we felt the sentence of death.
But this happened that we might not rely on
ourselves but on God, who raises the dead.

—2 CORINTHIANS 1:9

∽

Lord, when I ponder my humanity, my mortality, it is easy to become stressed about my limitations. People around me seek ways to live forever, yet they are missing the truth of Your gift. I am so thankful I have received Your Son and eternity. Now, please guide me to trust this gift. Give my heart assurance that today is about my life here on earth, and Your plan for my tomorrow is also in the works.

God, I rely on Your provision to make it through daily life. Remind my spirit to have this same reliance on Your provision of eternal life.

Nothing Can Stop Me Now

He will have no fear of bad news; his heart is steadfast, trusting in the LORD.

—PSALM 112:7

❧

Lord, lately I have been waiting for the proverbial other shoe to drop. I faced some difficulties, and now I am afraid to trust You with what could happen next. My body feels tight with anticipation of further hardship rather than blessing.

The world tells me that struggle is a sign of weakness or is the fruit of failure. But because I know You and Your ways, I understand how trials are blessings. My dependence on You becomes a life of freedom. I am moving forward today. I trust Your will, Lord.

Truth Leads to Trust

Love does not delight in evil but rejoices with the truth. It always protects, always trusts, always hopes, always perseveres.

—1 CORINTHIANS 13:6-7

❧

God, in my relationships with other people, help me present You truthfully. I want my family to be able to trust me completely. I pray I will always be able, with Your strength, to protect them, give them hope, and lead them through the hard times. When they turn to me for reassurance, may I turn their hearts to Your hope.

I do not know any way through this life except to follow You each day. You guide my steps. Sometimes they are steps meant for me alone. At other times they are steps intended to set the way for other people. Lord, find my heart trusting and my spirit willing.

Real Manhood

Learning from Others

Uzziah was sixteen years old when he became
king, and he reigned in Jerusalem fifty-two years.
His mother's name was Jecoliah; she was from
Jerusalem. He did what was right in the eyes of
the LORD, just as his father Amaziah had done.
He sought God during the days of Zechariah, who
instructed him in the fear of God. As long as he
sought the LORD, God gave him success.

—2 CHRONICLES 26:3-5

❧

I pray to understand the importance of being a man…a man of God. I turn to You with my needs, my praises, my thanksgiving. Yet I often turn to ungodly examples of manhood. There are so many images and idols that sway my good intentions from Your will to false truths.

Direct me toward mentorship with a godly man. Give me discernment as I weigh the choices of my life. I pray for Your leading so I can read words written by men of God, listen to the lessons of these men, and emulate those who live a righteous, holy life. I long to be the man You created me to be.

Just Look at My Father

This is the written account of Adam's line. When God created man, he made him in the likeness of God.

—GENESIS 5:1

⌇

Lord, what do You see in me that reflects You? As I go about my day, are there moments when You shine through? I pray this is so. Have my many efforts to succeed as a man steered me away from my Father's ways? Lord, lead me back on track. Present me with the challenge to become more like You in all things.

Right now I need patience and understanding. I need reassurance of my Father's love. You have blessed me in so many ways. Let me count these blessings and pray over my life so that the security of Your love fills my heart. Thank You for caring about me, for creating me and providing Your Son as a model of manhood and godliness.

I Am a Son

Because you are sons, God sent the Spirit of his Son into our hearts, the Spirit who calls out, "Abba, Father." So you are no longer a slave, but a son; and since you are a son, God has made you also an heir.

—GALATIANS 4:6-7

∽

How I want to resemble my heavenly Father! Lord, as You formed man and woman, what did You wish for Your children? I want to live my life in a way that is pleasing to You. I want to walk and talk with the grace and wisdom of Abba. Open my eyes to how I can be more like You during times of rest, in moments of interaction, and at points of decision.

My earthly father has taught me many things. As I continue to grow in my adult life, I look to You to teach me the ways of heaven and holiness.

Caring for My Life

*Show me, O LORD, my life's end and the number
of my days; let me know how fleeting is my life.
You have made my days a mere handbreadth; the
span of my years is as nothing before you. Each
man's life is but a breath.*

—PSALM 39:4-5

∾

God, it is so amazing how I can rest in the truth that
my life is just a breath in Your eternal plan. But I do
find peace in this understanding. It means my days are
part of a whole picture. I am insignificant compared to
Your greatness, but I am significant because I am Yours.
My days count in the unfolding of mankind. My family
history and my family's future are connected to Your
master plan.

With each breath I take into my lungs, fill me with
the desire to care for my life. I want to consider it precious and meaningful. Show me how to please You,
Lord, with all that I have and with all that I am.

Vocation

Future Plans

For we are God's workmanship, created in Christ Jesus to do good works, which God prepared in advance for us to do.

—EPHESIANS 2:10

❧

My finger is double-jointed. My face shows the wear of past years. My voice is used to praise You. You know and see all of this because I am the creation of Your hands. My heart beats in a rhythm designed by You. Use me, Lord. Lead me toward the good works You wish to entrust to this child.

As You formed me, You blessed me with plans for a future. I don't want to miss out on any of the exciting changes, opportunities, and blessings You have in store for me. Where I am resistant to follow, Lord, give me a change of mind and heart. Draw my spirit closer to the Spirit so I walk in communion with Christ.

Show Me the Purpose

So neither he who plants nor he who waters is
anything, but only God, who makes things grow.
The man who plants and the man who waters have
one purpose, and each will be rewarded according
to his own labor. For we are God's fellow workers;
you are God's field, God's building.

—1 CORINTHIANS 3:7-9

∽

Show me the purpose, Lord. When I head to work
or return home, fill me with Your wisdom. When I am
centered in Your will, I feel it, Lord. It doesn't mean that
all is going well. In fact, I have found my trust strengthened during the trials. Don't let me give up on the calling
You have prepared for me.

As I work with other people, let me reflect on their
purpose and contribution. Let me praise them for their
good works and thank You for their efforts. We are all
a part of the body You have formed. Led by Christ, we
are called to find the way of righteousness and integrity.
I make this my goal and my pledge to You, Lord.

Prize in Sight

Brothers, I do not consider myself yet to have taken hold of it. But one thing I do: Forgetting what is behind and straining toward what is ahead, I press on toward the goal to win the prize for which God has called me heavenward in Christ Jesus.

—PHILIPPIANS 3:13-14

✍

I have returned to my past recently for a visit. For days I have been carrying around some regrets that I thought I had given over to You long ago. I don't want to spend time with these ghosts, Lord. I want to leave the past behind me and press on toward the goal of purpose.

I know that I cannot fully embrace the next step in my life until I release my past worries to Your care. I do not look at my faith as a system of rewards, but I do see the prize of eternity ahead. It glimmers and reflects Your radiant grace. It inspires me to be steady, hardworking, and aware of Your calling every day.

The Job of Holiness

*As obedient children, do not conform to the evil
desires you had when you lived in ignorance. But just
as he who called you is holy, so be holy in all you do;
for it is written: "Be holy, because I am holy."*

—1 PETER 1:14-16

✍

This holiness thing is work. I am forgiven because of
Your grace. I did nothing to earn that gift. But the quest
for holiness is not easy. I am paring away the places of my
life that counter this purpose. I have had to step away from
former associates who brought me down. You revealed a
sin in my life that was blocking my growth. I am understanding that this pursuit will indeed involve effort.

Keep me pure and energized, Lord. I want to be up
for the task and ready for the challenges You place before
me.

Freedom

I Am in a Jam

Listen to my cry, for I am in desperate need;
rescue me from those who pursue me, for they are
too strong for me. Set me free from my prison,
that I may praise your name.

—PSALM 142:6-7

∽

My enemies might not resemble those faced by biblical warriors, but I do have enemies. There are attackers of my time, my well-being, my happiness. The quest for money, jealousy, blind ambition, reckless talk...these enemies stalk my spirit and wear it down. I feel the oppression in my gut. Some of these enemies were as familiar as friends, so it was hard to turn from them. I realize I have not moved far enough away and am vulnerable.

Help me use Your strength to fight these lurking foes, Lord. Arm me with Your Word, Your truth, and Your peace. I will praise Your name.

The Harm of Want

Keep your lives free from the love of money and be content with what you have, because God has said, "Never will I leave you; never will I forsake you."

—HEBREWS 13:5

❧

If someone asked me point-blank, "Would you trade the security of God's presence for the security of great wealth?" I would say no. Yet, Lord, I find that my daily decisions reflect the opposite of that adamant no. I am lacking contentment in my life right now. I am easily displeased when plans for my money and possessions are ruined.

God, direct my decisions and my heart so that my life is in line with Your will. I will only find freedom when I release the burden of material accumulation into Your hands. Let me discover the joy found in what You want for my life.

Not for Sale

The Spirit and the bride say, "Come!" And let him
who hears say, "Come!" Whoever is thirsty, let
him come; and whoever wishes, let him take the
free gift of the water of life.

—REVELATION 22:17

✍

In this culture of comparison shopping and making deals, Your gift of eternal life is easy to question. I'm sorry, Lord, but it is difficult to truly "sell" a real deal anymore without provoking skepticism. We are trained to doubt something that is too good to be true. And surely the gift of life is that. What we forget is that You are not too good to be true; You are the Spirit of goodness, the Creator of kindness and mercy.

God, help me show other people how genuine Your gift is. If they do not see evidence of Your salvation in my life, they will forever question the authenticity of my claims. I want to become the one who invites other people to drink of Your mercy absolutely free of charge.

The Prison of Judgment

Do not judge, and you will not be judged. Do not condemn, and you will not be condemned. Forgive, and you will be forgiven. Give, and it will be given to you. A good measure, pressed down, shaken together and running over, will be poured into your lap. For with the measure you use, it will be measured to you.

—LUKE 6:37-38

❧

Lord, when did You put me in charge of judging all my brothers in Christ? Never. That is what I thought. So why do I pretend to sit on a higher moral ground than other people? God, this is a lonely place to be anyway. I don't want to be eager to tear down another child of God. I want to be a builder of Your kingdom.

Free me from the prison of my judgment so that I can receive and share Your grace. I want to give a good measure of grace so I can in turn receive a good measure back from Your heart.

Fatherhood

A God for
All Generations

May the LORD our God be with us as he was with our fathers; may he never leave us nor forsake us. May he turn our hearts to him, to walk in all his ways and to keep the commands, decrees and regulations he gave our fathers.

—1 KINGS 8:57-58

෨෨

You are the God of my father and of those men in my life whom I count as mentors. I thank You for the gift of salvation that ties me to prior generations. As I reflect on my lineage, I know it is not the blood of my family line that makes me who I am, but the blood of Christ.

God, give me a heart for You that beats so strong and so pure that it resounds in my children. Let my legacy be one of faith. Order my priorities so my children feel precious and loved, so I can introduce them to what it feels like to be Your child.

A Daily Choice

*Fix these words of mine in your hearts and minds;
tie them as symbols on your hands and bind them
on your foreheads. Teach them to your children,
talking about them when you sit at home and
when you walk along the road, when you lie down
and when you get up.*

—DEUTERONOMY 11:18-19

∞

Being a good father is a daily choice, Lord—or rather, a string of choices. I practice the art of patience, the discipline of disciplining, and the forced skill of multitasking all before breakfast. I rely on the wisdom of Your Word to show me how to interact with my children in a godly way. I share verses with them so they, too, can understand my Source of knowledge and peace.

Being a father and being a child of God require the same degree of attention and priority. My diligence in growing my faith directly affects my efforts to grow my children. Lord, thank You for the model of Your fatherly love.

Staying Pure

I will walk in my house with blameless heart.
I will set before my eyes no vile thing.

—PSALM 101:2-3

∽

Keep me pure, Lord. There are many distractions in the world today. The vices of many people are presented as not only okay but healthy. There is such a discrepancy between society's standards and Your own. Help me guard my heart and life from sinful desires so I can enter my home and return to my family with a clean, righteous spirit.

Building a family requires great trust. Lord, may my family always be able to depend on me to be a man of integrity, vulnerability, and honesty. As You hear my requests for forgiveness, Lord, protect me so I can remain blameless and worthy of my loving family.

Team Teaching

All your sons will be taught by the LORD, and
great will be your children's peace.

—ISAIAH 54:13

∽

God, last week I faced a moment when I just didn't feel adequate to be guiding my children through life. There are so many things I do not understand about the world and about how You work in the world. The question that filled me with worry was, "What if they need help or answers that I am not able to give them?"

Then You reminded me that You, too, have a vested interest in the lives of my children. My children are Your children. Your concern for their knowledge and fulfillment surpasses even my own. My job is not to be their only teacher, but to direct them in all ways to You, the Creator and Teacher of all good things.

Integrity

Live and Learn

*He who ignores discipline despises himself, but
whoever heeds correction gains understanding.
The fear of the LORD teaches a man wisdom, and
humility comes before honor.*

—PROVERBS 15:32-33

⤜⤝

Lord, open my heart up to correction. When I receive
fair guidance from another person, I become defensive
or embarrassed. I hold back from saying anything about
my feelings, but later I dwell on that sense of failure
rather than on the tools I have been given to do a better
job. Let me trust that Your hand is on me and the circumstances so I will be receptive to the lessons You are
teaching me.

God, I want to be a humble man with integrity in
all areas of my life. Let me be as eager to receive instruction as I am to receive praise. The next time I face this
situation, I will lean on You for strength.

Starving the Ego

*It is not good to eat too much honey, nor is it
honorable to seek one's own honor. Like a city
whose walls are broken down is a man who lacks
self-control.*

—PROVERBS 25:27-28

᭒

Oh, Lord. As I experience success in different ways,
I pray I will always give You the glory. Keep my head
level. Help me not to become bloated with pride and
false importance. It is so easy to feed on the sweetness
of compliments rather than on the hard kernels of Your
truth.

God, build up my self-control so I am protected from
the desire to stuff my ego with empty words. I pray that
You see me as a person of substance and integrity. Let
my honor come from my association with the King of
kings.

Moving Toward Good Things

For the LORD God is a sun and shield; the LORD
bestows favor and honor; no good thing does he
withhold from those whose walk is blameless.

—PSALM 84:11

✐

God, Giver of all that is good, You are the Source of the grace that flows through my veins and keeps me alive. Your strength moves me toward good things. I work to hold my head up high, not with pride, but with honor that comes from the faith life.

Keep me in line with Your will. Push, tug, and lead me toward the future You have for me. When I am not making progress toward Your blessings, it is not because You are withholding them. It is because I have not yet moved toward Your will. Do not let me stray from the goodness that awaits, Lord.

Success

Money Versus Value

What good is it for a man to gain the whole world,
and yet lose or forfeit his very self?

—LUKE 9:25

⚜

Lord, I caught myself planning how my money could multiply over the years, and not once did I think about Your provision and plan. Please help me to find a balance as I strive for success. Present me with Your definition of successful living so I do not equate my earnings and my future portfolio with true value.

I have seen how money destroys people. God, do not let me rest in monetary securities. You are my Provider and the Creator of my life strategy. May I become excited as I imagine how my current blessings will multiply as I learn to trust You.

Take the High Road

*"For my thoughts are not your thoughts, neither
are your ways my ways," declares the Lord. "As
the heavens are higher than the earth, so are my
ways higher than your ways and my thoughts than
your thoughts."*

—ISAIAH 55:8-9

∽

My earthly perspective is in the trenches right now.
Lord, pull me out of this place and lift my thoughts to
a higher plane so I begin to see life as You do. What
started as a rut became a chasm that limited my ability
to succeed or move forward in Your will. Please forgive
me for thinking You would be limited by the walls of
that trench. I forgot that You are God.

When You bring me home to heaven, I will already
know the feeling of rising above my human circumstances, because today You lifted me up and showed me,
once again, that You are my God.

Practice Makes Perfect

*So if you have not been trustworthy in handling worldly
wealth, who will trust you with true riches? And if you
have not been trustworthy with someone else's
property, who will give you property of your own?*

—LUKE 16:11-12

✑

In my early years of adulthood, I was not a very
good steward, Lord. You had given me numerous blessings, opportunities, and elements of value which I
abused or squandered. Then I had years of want and
regret. Now I see Your hand guiding me once again
toward success and ownership. You do not call me to
great wealth, but now I understand how to be a steward
of each and every blessing.

God, let me seek wise counsel in matters of money
and property so I can serve You and Your body with
such blessings. And may I always seek Your counsel as
I make decisions about the biggest blessing of all: the
gift of life.

Building a Life

Now, my son, the LORD be with you, and may you have success and build the house of the LORD your God, as he said you would. May the LORD give you discretion and understanding when he puts you in command over Israel, so that you may keep the law of the LORD your God.

—1 CHRONICLES 22:11-12

✍

I have heard many speakers on the topics of success and life management. Those that have the most influence on me are those who are unknowingly borrowing material from the true source: You and Your Word. Even non-Christians understand the importance of starting with a solid foundation to build a solid life.

God, make my life a house of the Lord. Guide me to use strong, worthy materials as I heed Your instruction for each step. The process involves determination, prayer, and sweat. But because my Cornerstone is Christ, this is a life worth building.

True Strength

Giving In and Getting Strong

Love the LORD your God with all your heart and with all your soul and with all your strength.

—DEUTERONOMY 6:5

∽

As a guy, I once equated love with weakness. I guess that came from the idea of going "weak in the knees" or "falling head over heels." But, God, it was finding and accepting Your love that changed my view of human love.

Giving up control and giving in to Your love became the start of true strength in my life. Opening up my heart and soul to Your love allowed me to lean upon Your understanding and will. Standing alone without the structure of faith is weakness. Thank You for a new definition and understanding of strength.

Weakness Works

When I came to you, brothers, I did not come with eloquence or superior wisdom as I proclaimed to you the testimony about God. For I resolved to know nothing while I was with you except Jesus Christ and him crucified. I came to you in weakness and fear, and with much trembling. My message and my preaching were not with wise and persuasive words, but with a demonstration of the Spirit's power, so that your faith might not rest on men's wisdom, but on God's power.

—1 CORINTHIANS 2:1-5

ॐ

People fear public speaking, and I don't blame them, Lord. There seems to be nothing worse than fumbling through words while the eyes of many people focus on me. I need to think about my status as a humble messenger in life. You can speak through my words and my actions if I give myself over to You.

I will accept this role of messenger and present what I need to say in my very human, imperfect way, because my weakness magnifies Your greatness. My humanity allows Your divinity to shine forth.

He Is Strong

But he said to me, "My grace is sufficient for you, for my power is made perfect in weakness." Therefore I will boast all the more gladly about my weaknesses, so that Christ's power may rest on me. That is why, for Christ's sake, I delight in weaknesses, in insults, in hardships, in persecutions, in difficulties. For when I am weak, then I am strong.

—2 CORINTHIANS 12:9-10

∽

I am weak, but You are strong. Yes, Jesus loves me, and I love Him. While having a list of weaknesses a mile long is not always a comforting thought, I finally understand why I am human and You are God. I don't like to shine a light on my failings, but I have learned to release them to You so You can use them to reveal Your might.

Thank You for giving me the freedom to have my identity in You. This allows me to showcase my weaknesses, give You credit for my moments of strength, and direct attention to Your grace. It is not about me. It is about You working through me. And as I rid myself of ego, I can be filled by the power of Your Spirit.

I've Got the Power

And we pray this in order that you may live a life worthy of the Lord and may please him in every way: bearing fruit in every good work, growing in the knowledge of God, being strengthened with all power according to his glorious might so that you may have great endurance and patience, and joyfully giving thanks to the Father, who has qualified you to share in the inheritance of the saints in the kingdom of light.

—COLOSSIANS 1:10-12

∽

God, I praise You for the life You have given me. When it bears fruit, it is because Your power has made it capable of goodness. If a pleasing harvest is brought forth from my life, I have energy and health in my body and spirit. I feel the power of You moving through me and my circumstances in order to bring Your plan to fruition.

My inheritance is a bountiful landscape. And in times of drought, I don't need to ask whether to continue working the fields. You call me to be strong...but not strong and alone, for I have Your power in my life to carry me through all seasons.

Management

All in the Family

*He must manage his own family well and see that
his children obey him with proper respect. (If
anyone does not know how to manage his own
family, how can he take care of God's church?)*

—1 TIMOTHY 3:4-5

❧

God, the family unit is my measure of true success.
How I am doing within and for my family directly relates
to how successful I am in other areas. If I power my way
through the business world, yet do not have the respect
of my children, I am not a man of stature but am a
failure. God, forgive me if I am ever tempted to choose
worldly success over the well-being of my family.

I pray for my friends who struggle with their home
life. It gives them an even sharper, more desperate edge
in the workplace. But the efforts of their hands and
minds become a house of cards instead of a substantial
offering of stone. Lord, encourage me and my friends to
put first things first and manage our homes in a way that
is pleasing to You.

If They Could
See Me Now

*For though I am absent from you in body, I am
present with you in spirit and delight to see how
orderly you are and how firm your faith in Christ is.*

—COLOSSIANS 2:5

∾

God, if my mentors and encouragers of the past
could see my life now, would they be pleased? Those
people who helped me grow in my faith early on...would
they be delighted by how I manage everything from
home to work to relationships? I pray to be able to
observe my life from a distance once in a while so I can
notice the areas where I need You all the more.

I pray my life is firmly in order. As I pray for this
structure, I also pray that I am willing to change course
at a moment's notice if it is Your will. Those who touched
my life in the past would not want me to ever put my
plans before Your own. I long to please You, Lord.

Pick Me

The Lord answered, "Who then is the faithful and wise manager, whom the master puts in charge of his servants to give them their food allowance at the proper time? It will be good for that servant whom the master finds doing so when he returns."

—LUKE 12:42-43

✍

Okay, God. I have been known to bite off more than I can chew. One success can go to my head so fast that I forget to thank You for the milestone and ask how to best use it. I pray You understand my eagerness to accomplish things. I pray You see through my childish impatience and look at my potential ability to serve You well.

I set my sights on work that pleases You. I do not earn Your grace, Lord, but I want to be worthy of the moment when You choose me to handle a responsibility. If You entrust me with an opportunity to do good, may You not be disappointed.

Part of a Whole

Now the body is not made up of one part but of many. If the foot should say, "Because I am not a hand, I do not belong to the body," it would not for that reason cease to be part of the body. And if the ear should say, "Because I am not an eye, I do not belong to the body," it would not for that reason cease to be part of the body....But in fact God has arranged the parts in the body, every one of them, just as he wanted them to be.

—1 CORINTHIANS 12:14-18

∽

God, the best managers are those who acknowledge the worth and contribution of every person they supervise. The best coaches are those who observe and utilize the strengths of every team member. Give me this mindset when I am put in charge of shepherding any group. Whether I am serving on a committee at church or participating in a workplace discussion, let me clearly see the value of each person there.

You see the beauty and originality of all of us, Lord. May I have Your eyes when looking into the eyes of another person. And then let me notice how that person resembles You.

Leading

The Way Everlasting

Search me, O God, and know my heart; test me and know my anxious thoughts. See if there is any offensive way in me, and lead me in the way everlasting.

—PSALM 139:23-24

∽

Do I offend You in any way, Lord? When I read the Old Testament, it seems Your followers were eager to have their hearts known and their evil ways pointed out. Call me to this place of willingness, God. I am reluctant to know my faults, so it is difficult to ask You to make them apparent. Yet, I want to be a healthy, informed servant so I can be led.

So lead me, Lord, to the way everlasting. Along the journey, reveal to me the secrets of my heart that even I do not know. Unveil the sins that keep me from better days.

Follow the Leader

Teach me to do your will, for you are my God;
may your good Spirit lead me on level ground.

—PSALM 143:10

❧

Lord, where You lead, I will follow. I pray that You will take me from the slippery slope of my way and direct me toward the level landscape of Your will. Each day I want to seek Your teaching.

Let the lessons You have for me be apparent in the moment You are presenting them. Where I can learn from my past, please help me reflect on those times and heal so I can be whole, healthy, and ready to receive whatever is next.

What It Takes

*Then he said to the crowd, "If any of you wants
to be my follower, you must put aside your
selfish ambition, shoulder your cross daily, and
follow me. If you try to keep your life for
yourself, you will lose it. But if you give up your
life for me, you will find true life."*

—LUKE 9:23-24 NLT

❧

Lord, You require me to leave behind my selfish
ways and carry my cross in order to follow You. In con-
temporary times, this is a difficult concept. In my life,
following can involve little commitment. I follow certain
trends and then lose interest. I follow a leading sports
team until the season is over. I follow teachings of my
youth until they conflict with my adult pursuits.

But being one of Your children is a decision which
involves my today, my tomorrow, and my eternity. Your
mercy calls me and inspires me to give up my life. This
is not a temporary interest; this is a passionate pursuit.

Model Behavior

*Therefore, as God's chosen people, holy and
dearly loved, clothe yourselves with compassion,
kindness, humility, gentleness and patience. Bear
with each other and forgive whatever grievances
you may have against one another. Forgive as
the Lord forgave you.*

—COLOSSIANS 3:12-13

∝

God, when You place me in the presence of other
people, I have a chance to lead by example...Your
example. Give me a heart of compassion and kindness
so I can reach out to other people with Your love. Grace
me with patience and gentleness so I can reflect Your
tenderness. And humble me before men so You are
exalted.

When my own pride or agenda gets in the way of
expressing You and Your feelings toward mankind,
please correct me. Convict my spirit so I can repent. And
with You as my witness, may I lead with a spirit of forgiveness to model Your greatest gift.

Marriage

Keeping the Faith

*Another thing you do: You flood the LORD's altar
with tears. You weep and wail because he no longer
pays attention to your offerings or accepts them
with pleasure from your hands. You ask, "Why?" It
is because the LORD is acting as the witness between
you and the wife of your youth, because you have
broken faith with her, though she is your partner,
the wife of your marriage covenant.*

—MALACHI 2:13-14

❧

Lord, You hold my marriage up to see if it is holy
and pleasing. You consider my actions toward my wife
and consider this partnership to be sacred. When I am
not caring for my wife as I should, You do not wish to
hear my pleas for attention or fulfillment. If I shame my
household, I have shamed You.

Create in me a giving, nurturing spirit toward my
wife. May I respect her, adore her, and cherish her.
Guard my heart so I never put this relationship at risk.
As You watch me, Lord, may my words and deeds
reflect faithfulness so I honor You and the wife of my
youth forever.

Helpmates

*Husbands, love your wives, just as Christ loved the
church and gave himself up for her to make her
holy, cleansing her by the washing with water
through the word, and to present her to himself as
a radiant church, without stain or wrinkle or any
other blemish, but holy and blameless.*

—EPHESIANS 5:25-27

ॐ

God, You created Eve to be Adam's helpmate. You
saw that Adam would not be whole, would not be fulfilled without the one designed to complete him. Thank
You, Lord, for establishing this relationship. I pray that
I stay devoted to my wife, my companion, and love her
without reservation.

I pray to be a caring, attentive man. Lord, keep me
from ever causing my wife to sin. May my behavior keep
her pure and radiant. May my words encourage and
strengthen her faith in You. Lead me in Your ways so
my commitment is righteous and never self-serving.
Thank You for the love of my life.

Me, My Wife, and Thee

Two are better than one, because they have a good return for their work: If one falls down, his friend can help him up. But pity the man who falls and has no one to help him up!...A cord of three strands is not quickly broken.

—ECCLESIASTES 4:9-10,12

᷇

Dear Lord, let me take the vows and ties of marriage seriously. This is such a big decision in my life. May I see, with Your eyes, the importance of such a covenant. I have spent many days on my own, enjoying solitude and the freedom of making decisions that primarily affect me. But I have also spent time thinking about how much stronger I would feel once I enter into a forever relationship.

When husbands and wives stay tethered to the cord of Your heartstrings, it becomes a strong lifeline. I want my spirit to be united in marriage, in faith, and in Your will, Lord.

Connection

Bad Connections

*Do not let anyone who delights in false humility
and the worship of angels disqualify you for the
prize. Such a person goes into great detail about
what he has seen, and his unspiritual mind puffs
him up with idle notions. He has lost connection
with the Head, from whom the whole body,
supported and held together by its ligaments and
sinews, grows as God causes it to grow.*

—COLOSSIANS 2:18-19

∽

So often my mind will separate from the actions of
my body, enlarging the gap between my will and Your
will, Father. My head knows of Your will, but my body
seems to disconnect and follow its own will. This loss
of connection between my understanding and my action
hurtles me through the gauntlet of frustration. The distance between me and You grows.

Eternal God, I pray for the restoration of my connection with You. Give me the spiritual wisdom to reclaim
that glorious peace found in abiding in Your will.

Resurrection of Relationship

So, my brothers, you also died to the law through the body of Christ, that you might belong to another, to him who was raised from the dead, in order that we might bear fruit to God.

—ROMANS 7:4

∽

The law calls to my attention rules, rules, and more rules simply to be obeyed. I become so obsessed with keeping and not breaking them that I have turned myself inward. I have become self-centered and have lost sight of my relationship with my Lord. The pain in my heart makes me long for the times when I had more hope.

O Lord, Your unselfishness gave us the power of the resurrection in Jesus. I pray for a reconnection with my Savior. Fill me again with the new life of the Spirit and lead me away from my selfish ways.

Connections

*From one man he made every nation of men, that they
should inhabit the whole earth; and he determined the
times set for them and the exact places where they
should live. God did this so that men would seek him
and perhaps reach out for him and find him, though he
is not far from each one of us. "For in him we live and
move and have our being." As some of your own poets
have said, "We are his offspring."*

—ACTS 17:26-28

‰

When I take my daily drive to work, I forget to notice
Your presence in all of Your creations. How can those
other drivers (especially the ones that ride my bumper
or run the yellow lights) be children of Your creation?
Why do I find myself so out of touch with Your other
children? I forget that each one is created in Your image,
and I become upset by their actions. I don't stop and
think long enough to have a heart for them.

Lord of all creation and all people, I open myself to
the workings of Your Spirit. Connect me to all of Your
children. I dedicate myself to seeing Your touch in the
world about me. With Your strength I will try to connect
with everyone I meet this day.

Fellowship and Faith

We proclaim to you what we have seen and heard, so that you also may have fellowship with us. And our fellowship is with the Father and with his Son, Jesus Christ. We write this to make our joy complete.

—1 JOHN 1:3-4

❧

Scripture calls me to the joy of fellowship with other people, Jesus. It is so easy to become busy with trivial things and disconnect from people. If only I could realize that life without fellowship is unlivable, lonely, and not as You intended it to be for me. A solitary existence would limit my exposure to Your character and compassion as You express it through other individuals in the body of Christ.

God, I feel the need to connect with other people and with You. I pray for the strength to do so. I ask Your help in prioritizing my activities today so that I may experience fellowship with other believers. May my joy be complete.

Worry

Pass On the Cheer

*An anxious heart weighs a man down, but a kind
word cheers him up.*

—PROVERBS 12:25

∾

My God and Savior, I tremble with fear of what other
people may think. And when someone expresses criticism
or judgment toward me, I manage to wear my mask of
indifference that hides the turmoil boiling inside. If only
people knew the damage they do with their thoughtless
words. I come to You with my pain, but I am unable to
share my feelings with anyone else.

Lord, I know there are so many times when I speak
without thinking and see the anguish in another person's
eyes. Please, God, help me to find the good and kind
word that will bring cheer to another. Then may I know
peace through the joy of other people.

Giving Doubt a Rest

*What does a man get for all the toil and anxious
striving with which he labors under the sun? All
his days his work is pain and grief; even at night
his mind does not rest....A man can do nothing
better than to eat and drink and find satisfaction
in his work. This too, I see, is from the hand of
God....To the man who pleases him, God gives
wisdom, knowledge and happiness.*

—ECCLESIASTES 2:22-26

❦

Oh, God, how many times do I toss and turn
throughout the night wondering what I am doing? Why
continue this constant cycle of effort and work? What
am I missing? Surely there must be more than this!
Where is the payoff? What about my reward?

Fill me with your Holy Spirit; ease my restless mind.
Free me from these chains of worry and doubt! Father,
please help me to enjoy each moment from day to day.
Hold me steady to the task at hand so that I discover the
satisfaction of a job well done. I thirst for Your wisdom and
yearn for the day my mind rests in Your faithfulness.

In God I Trust

*Therefore I tell you, do not worry about your life,
what you will eat or what you will drink, or about
your body, what you will wear....And can any of
you by worrying add a single hour to your span of
life?...Your heavenly Father knows that you need
all these things. But strive first for the kingdom of
God and his righteousness, and all these things
will be given to you as well.*

—MATTHEW 6:25,27,32-33 (NRSV)

✐

Lord, it's so hard *not* to focus on money. Sitting here at the kitchen table, I end up making myself sick with worry over these bills. It's never enough, Lord. What if something bad happens? What if I lose my job? What if the market crashes and we lose our retirement money? Our savings account would only last so long. Then what, Lord?

Dear gracious God, forgive me for not trusting You. Please strengthen my faith and help me to remember that no matter what situation life finds me in, You will be there with me. Despite my misgivings I need not worry, for Your will shall be done.

Fearless

*Yet if you devote your heart to him and stretch out
your hands to him, if you put away the sin that is in
your hand and allow no evil to dwell in your tent, then
you will lift up your face without shame; you will stand
firm and without fear. You will surely forget your
trouble, recalling it only as waters gone by. Life will be
brighter than noonday, and darkness will become like
morning. You will be secure, because there is hope; you
will look about you and take your rest in safety.*

—JOB 11:13-18

❧

God, I admit it: I get so caught up in the seeming
importance of day-to-day adversities that I forget to call
upon You. Opportunities to care for other people and
seek Your guidance slip by me. Then something happens, and it is crisis time again. That is when I turn to
You and plead for Your intervention. I promise to put
Your will first, but this good intention doesn't last.

Oh, Lord, fill me with Your Spirit today. Let Him
shake me to the core so that I think first of how You can
be served, letting all else fall into place. Guide me in my
day-to-day labors so my actions are led by You and my
heart is filled with Your love. Soothe my soul so I feel
secure walking along Your path.

Power

How to Be First

Jesus called them together and said, "You know that those who are regarded as rulers of the Gentiles lord it over them, and their high officials exercise authority over them. Not so with you. Instead, whoever wants to become great among you must be your servant, and whoever wants to be first must be slave of all. For even the Son of Man did not come to be served, but to serve, and to give his life as a ransom for many."

—MARK 10:42-45

⚬⁄⁄⁄⁄⁄

Dear Lord, thank You for helping me get to where I am today. I know that my life has been blessed with a number of successes. I admit that I like to do things my way. I don't like giving up control to someone else. I get so upset with people when they don't do as I say. I'm used to giving the orders, and I'm good at it. Please, God, help temper my small authority with humility and grace.

Almighty One, I am amazed at what Your Son was able to do for me. It is not easy to choose to be last. That competitive edge and drive to be first have been ingrained in me since my early years. Help me to find a way to put other people ahead of myself, to uplift my brothers and sisters, to be a true servant. Oh, Lord, help me resist having to be first.

Remind Me

But we have this treasure in jars of clay to show that this all-surpassing power is from God and not from us. We are hard pressed on every side, but not crushed; perplexed, but not in despair; persecuted, but not abandoned; struck down, but not destroyed. We always carry around in our body the death of Jesus, so that the life of Jesus may also be revealed in our body.

—2 CORINTHIANS 4:7-10

❧

Heavenly Father, remind me how much I live by Your power and not mine (although I admit that I don't really like the reminders—sometimes they overwhelm me). I know that when everything is going well, my pride can overtake me, and out comes my self-will.

Lord God, help me to remember that I don't have to do this all alone. Remind me to lean on Your power, to reach out for Jesus whenever I feel that I can no longer go the distance. Almighty God, help me to remember that Your power can lift me above any setback, and I have no need to fear.

Grace Is Enough

*Therefore, to keep me from being too elated, a
thorn was given me in the flesh.... Three times I
appealed to the Lord about this, that it would
leave me, but he said to me, "My grace is
sufficient for you, for power is made perfect in
weakness...." Therefore I am content.*

—2 CORINTHIANS 12:7-12 (NRSV)

෧

God, if anyone should have been able to pray away
physical pain, it would have been the saintly Paul. Alas,
the thorn remained. Sometimes healings take place, but
often pain remains. When I or a loved one suffers, I
wonder, "Should I have prayed harder?" You call me to
come to You with my requests, yet it is not my place to
dictate Your will in any situation.

Lord, empower me even though I contract thorns in
my flesh and am doubled over with pain. Help me to
find contentment when I experience Your grand power.
Enable me to carry on in spite of illness and hardship.
May I know Your grace is sufficient for me. Thanks be
to God!

Power Over Sin

Therefore rid yourselves of all sordidness and rank growth of wickedness, and welcome with meekness the implanted word that has the power to save your souls. But be doers of the word, and not merely hearers who deceive themselves.

—JAMES 1:21-22 (NRSV)

❧

Dear God, how easy it is to get sucked into the depravity of humanity. Temptations pull ever so gently; the pressure remains at every turn. Sin emerges on the television, in books, magazines, and movies. I am bombarded by ideas that counter the values You ask me to hold dear.

Lord, I welcome Your Word. Fill me with the power to not only withstand, but also to move forward in service as well. Let me be one who dares to be different. Give me the strength to show other people Your Word through my actions. May they come to know You when they see You in me. This is my prayer.

Covenant

Promises, Promises

*And God said, "This is the sign of the covenant I
am making between me and you and every living
creature with you, a covenant for all generations to
come: I have set my rainbow in the clouds, and it
will be the sign of the covenant between me and
the earth."*

—GENESIS 9:12-13

∾

Lord, at times the rush of events obscures my aware-
ness that this world is Your world, even with the traffic
jams, lost keys, tax forms, sick children, and backed-up
sinks. If only I could remember to stop and regroup
every time I saw one of Your rainbows.

Maker of heaven and earth, may I receive the grace
to keep both life and living in perspective. Beyond the
storms, I thank You for the quiet arch in full color that
expands over all You have created and stands as a
reminder of Your promise to us.

As for Me and My House

*But if serving the L*ORD *seems undesirable to you, then choose for yourselves this day whom you will serve, whether the gods your forefathers served beyond the River, or the gods of the Amorites, in whose land you are living. But as for me and my household, we will serve the L*ORD.

—JOSHUA 24:15

∽

Almighty God, there are times when I slip and slide. You know how many times I have failed You. Often I stumble when I try to serve more than one master. I choose to serve objects of desire rather than following Your will, Your calling for me, or Your precepts.

I yearn for the day when my faith will stand strong and my service rest secure. Hold me steady and keep my path straight and true as I choose again to serve only You. Let me pass along this conviction to my household. Let me lead by example and please You.

Write Your Will on My Heart

*This is the [new] covenant I will make with the
house of Israel....I will put my law in their minds
and write it on their hearts. I will be their God,
and they will be my people.*

—JEREMIAH 31:33

∽

Lord, if only I could have Your will and way so
written on my heart, in my inmost being, that I would
not have to ask, "Shall I do this, or shall I do that?" I
would know how to act without counting the cash or
seeking self-gain. How often do You long to write Your
will upon my life, yet come across my resistance, my
own strong will countering Your intention for good? You
call me to be Your own. Lord, help me run to Your side
and be named Your child, one of Your people.

I open my heart now to Your divine penmanship.
Lord, please write.

Friendship

The Freeing Friendship

You are my friends if you do what I command.

—JOHN 15:14

✍

Lord, I'm Your follower, but also Your friend. Help me see more clearly how to be a good friend by doing what You ask of me. My life is a gift from You, and I want to invest it to the best of my ability in doing the work to which You've called me.

I thank You that Your commands are not constraining, but freeing. In friendship with You, and in obedience to You, I find true joy.

Lord Jesus, I thank You for inviting me to be Your friend.

Keep Me Close, Lord

All the disciples deserted him and fled.
—MATTHEW 26:56

∽

The disciples—Your friends—heard You, loved You, followed You...and then deserted You when the going got tough. How that must have hurt. It's expected that our enemies will distance themselves from us...but we look to our friends to be there for us in the dark days. But Your friends were afraid and their fear drove them away from You.

Lord, I too, am Your disciple. I am Your friend. You have shown Yourself ever-present during my dark days, though sometimes *I'm* the one who wants to flee when the times get hard. Remind me, Lord, that running away from You is not the way to react to difficulties. In fact, when those things happen, Lord, draw me closer to You. Let me find myself strengthened by You, able to face the obstacles in my path.

Keep me close, Lord. Real close!

David and Jonathan

*After David had finished talking with Saul,
Jonathan became one in spirit with David, and he
loved him as himself. From that day Saul kept
David with him and did not let him return to his
father's house. And Jonathan made a covenant
with David because he loved him as himself.
Jonathan took off the robe he was wearing and
gave it to David, along with his tunic, and even his
sword, his bow and his belt.*

—1 SAMUEL 18:1-4

✍

Lord, much has been made about the friendship
between David and Jonathan. And truly they did have a
loyalty toward one another that I just don't often see in
today's busy world. Friendships like theirs must be something You alone can bring to pass. Truth be told, I could
use a close friend or two with whom I can really be
myself. Someone who will give me good advice when I
need it. Someone who will tell me when I'm off base or
taking the wrong path. And Lord, I'd like to be able to
be that friend to someone else too. I pray that You would
open the door for greater friendships in my life…even
deep friendships that will stand the test of time.

Cautious in Friendship

A righteous man is cautious in friendship, but the way of the wicked leads them astray.

—PROVERBS 12:26

✐

Lord, guard my friendships. Keep me from friendships with evil men. Remind me to be cautious with those who are not friends with You and who might cause me to compromise my faith or do that which does not honor You. I pray You'll present opportunities for me to share with these friends about the greatest Friend of all—You, Lord.

To those who You have placed in my life as friends, may I truly *be* their friend in every way I can. And may I never take the gift of friendship for granted.

Serving

Serving in Grace

*Each one should use whatever gift he has received
to serve others, faithfully administering God's
grace in its various forms.*

—1 PETER 4:10

❧

Thank You, God for my gifts of grace. Show me how to use them in the service of others today. Give me eyes to spot those to whom I can offer a word of hope or encouragement. Give me ears to hear the silent plea for help. Give me hands to reach out to those in need.

And, Lord, bring across my path today the people whom You have graced that can help me in my distress.

The God Who Sees

*Be sure to fear the LORD and serve him faithfully
with all your heart; consider what great things he
has done for you.*

—1 SAMUEL 12:24

✍

Oh Lord, You have indeed done great things for
me—many of which I probably don't even recognize.
Your eyes are ever upon me. You have seen my needs
even before I have and responded with abundance.
When I consider Your goodness to me, I can only offer
myself up to serve You with all my heart. Today is Yours,
Lord. Guide my steps. Open doors of service for me.
Teach me to fear You in love. Help me to remember
Your many goodnesses to me.

The Gift of Giving

Even the Son of Man did not come to be served, but to serve, and to give his life as a ransom for many.

—MARK 10:45

∽

The Christian life is about serving others, isn't it, Lord? By giving my life away to others, I give my life to You. That seems so right.

Lord, thank You for the example of giving You have set by ransoming my own life through the death of Your Son on the cross. Help to me remember that when I give to someone in need—even when it seems a sacrifice to me—that I'm giving to You...and following Your example.

Praise You, Father, for the gift of giving.

The Way Up Is Down

Whoever serves me must follow me; and where I am, my servant also will be. My Father will honor the one who serves me.

—JOHN 12:26

∽

Father, it excites me to know that when I serve, I will be where You are. I can be all You want me to be by simply giving myself away to others in their need. Thank You that there is honor from You in serving. Sometimes, Lord, I do seem to aspire to lofty positions where others will notice my work. Guard my heart against selfish ambition. Keep my heart away from desiring leadership as much as desiring servanthood. Truly in Your eyes, the way up is down.

Vision

Serving Before Kings

Do you see a man skilled in his work? He will serve before kings; he will not serve before obscure men.

—PROVERBS 22:29

✒

Father in heaven, thank You for giving me a work to do in this life. Help me to become even more skilled at Your calling for me. As others see the abilities You've given me, may they understand that those skills are truly a gift from above. May the work of my hands, mind, and body be glorifying to You, O Lord. May I be a good steward of the talents You've assigned to me and may they bear much fruit for You.

Noble Plans

The noble man makes noble plans, and by noble deeds he stands.

—ISAIAH 32:8

❧

God, I need help with my planning skills. So often it seems I just do the next necessary thing. The result is often just plugging through my work without focusing my eyes on the greater vision of my work. So much of what You would have me do is surely an incremental work: a little here, a little there—but always leading to a specific goal.

Show me, Lord, that goal. Give me *vision*. Help me plan to accomplish that vision through the strength You give me. Lord, *establish* the plans for my life and let nothing deter me from seeing them fulfilled.

The Desires of My Heart

*May he give you the desire of your heart and
make all your plans succeed.*

—PSALM 20:4

∽

What a joy to know, Father, that You delight to work through the godly desires of my heart. You show me how to move ahead with my life largely through the desires I have that conform to Your Word. I trust You, Lord, to move me on with my plans as they are rooted in You. Keep a guard over my desires that none of them become merely fleshly, ambitious goals of my own making. Plant within me a divine sense of mission for my desires. Water, O Lord, those plans and bring them to fruition.

Praise You, God, for choosing to work through me.

The Foolish Man

He said, "This is what I'll do. I will tear down my
barns and build bigger ones, and there I will store
all my grain and my goods."

—LUKE 12:18

∽

God, I know the foolish man only dreams to build a better life in *this* world. But You have called me to something greater. Your plans for me are eternal, Lord. Give me eyes to see the true riches of a life invested in You, and not in earthly securities. Help me resist the desire to be rich in this life at the neglect of my soul. Lord, I set all that aside and choose instead *Your* vision for my life.

Every day, Lord, it seems I read reports of those who are banking on this life alone. How foolish they are. Father, let every such report be a reminder that I choose not to build larger barns or to store additional grain…no, Lord, keep my investments in the divine depositories.

Eternity

Eternal Thanks

O LORD my God, I will give you thanks forever.
—PSALM 30:12

∽

Lord, I'm only too aware that Your universe could have done quite nicely without my existence. And yet, in Your divine plan, You included *me*. You created me in my mother's womb, You were there at my birth and all through my childhood…and then You sought me and saved me. You brought me to Yourself and poured Your love out on me. How can I then not offer eternal thanks? How can I not praise You for my creation? You are my God and I am Your son. Thank You, thank You, thank You.

The Path of Life

You have made known to me the path of life; you will fill me with joy in your presence, with eternal pleasures at your right hand.

—PSALM 16:11

∽

Thank You, Lord that I have eternal life in You. And even in this life You give me daily joy in Your presence. You sustain me with the power of Your right hand. And awaiting me are the eternal pleasures You've created for me to enjoy forever. Praise You for removing me from the path of death and setting my feet on the path of life. Thank You for the joy of Your presence…and for an eternity full of pleasure with You, my Father.

Lord, I Believe!

Whoever believes in the Son has eternal life.

—JOHN 3:36

∽

Lord, I believe! I believe in You and I believe in Your Son. And for such a simple faith, You have given me eternal life. That eternal life is not something I will someday inherit, it's mine right now and I rejoice in it. I also have eternal fellowship with You…even now, Lord. I am a blessed man, no matter what my day holds.

Thank You for the gift of eternal life. Thank You for Your Son. You are worthy of praise!

Eternity in My Heart

*He has made everything beautiful in its time. He has
also set eternity in the hearts of men; yet they cannot
fathom what God has done from beginning to end.*

—ECCLESIASTES 3:11

∽

God, I know full well that You have set eternity in
my heart. There is within me the knowledge that there's
so much more than this earthly life. Thank You for that
which is indeed beautiful in its time. You have set the
universe in motion and in so doing, have given me a
role to play…and a life in You to enjoy. I cannot fathom
it all, but I can believe it. I can trust. I can praise You…
and enjoy You.

Sexuality

A Good Thing

I tell you that anyone who looks at a woman lustfully has already committed adultery with her in his heart.

—MATTHEW 5:28

∽

Lord, You made me a male. With that comes certain desires that I know I must steward correctly. You created sexual desire with the intention that it be a *good* thing. All around me I see men who fail miserably on this issue of lust. It's powerful, Lord…and destructive. Help me guard my eyes and my heart from evil imaginations. Teach me to honor Your plan for sexuality and not allow it to be cheapened by the lusts of the world around me. Help me be strong with other men who have conquered this temptation. Give strength, O Lord.

Staying Pure

Flee from sexual immorality. All other sins a man commits are outside his body, but he who sins sexually sins against his own body.

—1 CORINTHIANS 6:18

∽

Father, I live in a world with easy access to sexual immorality. I could easily take advantage of the temptations surrounding me. It would not be hard. But, Lord, I know the results would be very hard indeed. I've seen the devastation that sexual immorality can bring to a man. I do not want that carnage in my life. Lord, help me to discern early when temptations to sexual immorality are at hand. Give me the power of Your Holy Spirit to resist this deadly sin. Keep my mind pure and my body under my control.

Not Even a Hint

Among you there must not be even a hint of sexual immorality.

—EPHESIANS 5:3

∽

I confess, Lord, that sometimes—perhaps even often—there is indeed the hint of sexual immorality in my thoughts—and potentially in my actions if I'm not on guard. Cleanse me from sexual sin and empower me against even the hint of immorality. Allow me, Father, to be known as a "safe" man. A man with whom any other person can be secure in knowing that I want no sexual favors from them. Allow me, too, Lord, to be an encouragement to other men who struggle with sexual temptations. Open the doors for honest sharing with other men that we might strengthen one another.

Holiness and Honor

It is God's will that you should be sanctified: that you should avoid sexual immorality; that each of you should learn to control his own body in a way that is holy and honorable, not in passionate lust like the heathen, who do not know God.

—1 THESSALONIANS 4:3-5

❧

God, I see that sexual immorality and unbridled passions are the marks of those who do not know You. May they, then, never be found in me—for I do know You. Help me to see the holiness and honor to be found in the controlling of my body. Teach me the ways of those who are sanctified—set apart for Your use. Thank You that Your will is for me to be safe from the destruction that comes with sexual immorality.

Health

Good Medicine

*A cheerful heart is good medicine, but a crushed
spirit dries up the bones.*

—PROVERBS 17:22

❧

Lord, sometimes my spirit is so dry I feel like I'm in
the middle of the Sahara. Lift my spirits, Father. Lighten
my heart. Give me Your joy, Your peace, Your spirit of
praise to overcome the heaviness. Help me get out of
myself and all the problems that are drying my spirit and
turn to You in rejoicing. All my happiness is found in
knowing You. Give me the medicine of a happy heart,
O Lord.

Health and Happiness

*My son, pay attention to what I say; listen closely to
my words. Do not let them out of your sight, keep
them within your heart; for they are life to those
who find them and health to a man's whole body.*

—PROVERBS 4:20-22

❧

Father God, Your Word gives me life. It gives me
both spiritual strength and physical power. Your words
are health to my body and my spirit. May Your truth
penetrate my whole being and keep me in health and
happiness. Allow Your Word to refresh me and give me
the vitality of a confident soldier.

Prospering Health

*Dear friend, I pray that you may enjoy good
health and that all may go well with you, even as
your soul is getting along well.*

—3 JOHN 1:2

⸎

God, I pray that You would prosper my body,
granting me good health, even as You prosper my soul.
Help me avoid that which would destroy my health—
whether junk food, bad attitudes, or laziness. Thank You
that You care about my health and all-around welfare.
You created this human body of mine and You know all
its intricacies. May my body be under Your care because
You are the one in whom I trust for my life. Every breath,
Lord, is a gift from You. I do not take it for granted.

Godly Appetites

*Their destiny is destruction, their god is their
stomach, and their glory is in their shame. Their
mind is on earthly things.*

—PHILIPPIANS 3:19

∽

Lord, You know about my appetites. Sometimes I
eat too much, sometimes I eat the wrong thing. Part of
it is time considerations. I simply don't take the time to
eat properly or get the exercise I need. And, yes, usually
it's because my mind is "on earthly things."

But, Father, I do not want my stomach to be my god,
for it will worsen my health. Help me instead to keep
You ever before me as my true God, the one I serve. Help
me to guard my health by guarding my appetites.

Work

My Measure of Creativity

*Moses said to the Israelites, "See, the LORD has chosen
Bezalel son of Uri, the son of Hur, of the tribe of Judah,
and he has filled him with the Spirit of God, with skill,
ability and knowledge in all kinds of crafts—to make
artistic designs for work in gold, silver and bronze, to cut
and set stones, to work in wood and to engage in all kinds
of artistic craftsmanship. And he has given both him and
Oholiab son of Ahisamach, of the tribe of Dan, the ability
to teach others. He has filled them with skill to do all
kinds of work as craftsmen, designers, embroiderers in
blue, purple and scarlet yarn and fine linen, and
weavers—all of them master craftsmen and designers."*

—EXODUS 35:30-35

✍

Father, it's amazing the way You give a measure of
creativity to every person. Even I have been given a measure of talent—and I praise You for my gifts. Help me
be a good steward of the skill, ability, and knowledge
You have given me. I pray You'd even multiply my talents
and my efforts. Give me a larger platform from which to
create. I pray You'd invest even greater creative energy
in me. Lord, I want to be the *best* I can be in all I do.
Grant me a great and useful imagination O Lord.

The Work of God Is This

*They asked him, "What must we do to do the
works God requires?" Jesus answered, "The work
of God is this: to believe in the one he has sent."*

—JOHN 6:28-29

❧

Of all the "work" required of man, there really is only
this one thing, Lord: to believe in Jesus, the One You
have sent. From that one act of believing, all the rest of
my work proceeds. It all has its root in You, Father.

I do believe in the One You've sent, Lord. I believe
in Jesus. There is no greater work I can do. Praise You
Lord for the simplicity there is in faith.

Profitable Work

*All hard work brings a profit, but mere talk leads
only to poverty.*

—PROVERBS 14:23

✌

Hard work, O Lord, is something I sometimes try to
avoid. And yet You have given each of us a work in
which we can be faithful and useful. Help me see more
clearly the ways my work can be more profitable for
Your kingdom. Keep a guard over my mouth lest all my
creativity be mere speculation and empty rhetoric. Let
diligence be the word that describes my work...and may
my diligence bring its due reward.

I'm His 24/7

Whatever you do, work at it with all your heart, as working for the Lord, not for men, since you know that you will receive an inheritance from the Lord as a reward. It is the Lord Christ you are serving.

—COLOSSIANS 3:23-24

∽

Sometimes, Lord, I only see my work as a separate part of who I am. But in reality, I'm Yours 24/7. I serve You in all I do. My work is for You, not for me, nor for my employer. You are the one I want to please with my efforts. May I be found faithful in the work given me.

And, Father, when I grumble over my work situation, remind me that such grumbling is really a bad attitude toward You. Help me remember to pray for those over me in my work.

Temptation

Deliver Me, Lord

Lead us not into temptation, but deliver us from the evil one.

—MATTHEW 6:13

❧

Lord, this is my prayer—that You keep me far from temptation. Deliver me from the sinful thoughts and actions that seem to pull me like a magnet. I see other men who surely triumph over their temptations, so I know it can be done. You *can* lead me away from temptation, Father. You *can* deliver me from the evil one.

Father, You have instructed me to pray that I do not fall into temptation. Given who I am and the temptations I face, that's truly my prayer now. Just as Jesus depended on You when He was sorely tempted in the desert, so do I depend on You in my hour of temptation.

Keep my eyes on the road to which You've called me—a road that passes right through all temptations unscathed.

You know how weak I can be, Lord. Your deliverance from temptation is my only hope. Do not fail me, Father!

A Covenant with My Eyes

I made a covenant with my eyes not to look lustfully at a girl.

—JOB 31:1

✑

Many of my temptations, Lord, enter through my eyes. I see something, and I want it. I covet it. And so I pursue it. Sometimes, Lord, those tempting thoughts have to do with lust. I visualize immoral sexual actions…and soon afterward I feel ashamed. Sometimes I *don't* feel ashamed. But You know, O Lord, and I have to believe You want me to overcome these thoughts…these lusts— both sexual and otherwise. Help me to keep a covenant with my eyes to resist evil thoughts when confronted with an opportunity to lust. Give me grace, Lord.

The Devil Must Flee

Submit yourselves, then, to God. Resist the devil,
and he will flee from you.

—JAMES 4:7

∽

Victory, Lord, comes through submitting to You. And in submitting to You, I must also resist the evil one. Your promise is that when I do resist, Satan will flee. So, Lord, I pray for two things: First, remind me early on when I need to resist, lest I be quickly overcome by the Enemy. Sometimes the temptation has already ensnared me before I think of resisting. Second, help me to remember that through You I do have the power to successfully resist the Enemy and that when I do, he MUST flee.

The Roaring Lion

Be self-controlled and alert. Your enemy the devil prowls around like a roaring lion looking for someone to devour. Resist him, standing firm in the faith, because you know that your brothers throughout the world are undergoing the same kind of sufferings.

—1 PETER 5:8-9

∽

When I'm tempted, God, it seems like I'm the only one who could be under such pressure to do what I know I shouldn't. But men all over the world—my brothers in Christ—are likewise tempted. Even down through history, good men have faced the very same temptations I do. Help me…and help my brothers in Christ…to stand firm in our faith in You. Help us to resist that roaring lion of temptation, the one who would devour me. Give me, O Father, the power of self-control and alertness.

Choices

Choosing Life

*If serving the LORD seems undesirable to you, then
choose for yourselves this day whom you will
serve, whether the gods your forefathers served
beyond the River, or the gods of the Amorites, in
whose land you are living. But as for me and my
household, we will serve the LORD.*

—JOSHUA 24:15

∽

Thank You, Father, for the gift of choice. You allow
me to choose the kind of life I will have by the choices
I make. As for my household—as for *me*—I choose to
serve You alone. I pray You'd send me reminders every
day of how choosing You is to play out in my daily life.
Make me continually aware of the wise and foolish
choices that are mine to make—and mostly to know
which is which.

Yes, Lord, I choose *You.*

The Mystery of God's Will

In his heart a man plans his course, but the LORD determines his steps.

—PROVERBS 16:9

༉

What a mystery Your will is, Lord! I pray, I make my plans and execute my choices…and yet because You are my sovereign Lord, You determine the outcome. What a great and wonderful source of confidence! You determine my steps! You have my back, Lord!

Thank You for working even my mistakes into a profitable outcome.

Praise You for Your excellent wisdom!

A or B?

If any of you lacks wisdom, he should ask God,
who gives generously to all without finding fault,
and it will be given to him. But when he asks, he
must believe and not doubt, because he who doubts
is like a wave of the sea, blown and tossed by the
wind. That man should not think he will receive
anything from the Lord; he is a double-minded
man, unstable in all he does.

—JAMES 1:5-8

∽

Lord, I often lack wisdom. Sometimes my choices are confusing. Should I choose A, or should I choose B? (Or C?)

I need Your insight, God. You have promised to give generous wisdom when I ask, and, Lord, I'm asking. Direct my steps. Help me have faith that what I hear and see is from You. I do not choose to be double-minded. I will trust You for wisdom. I will make choices in bold faith that You have granted me the wisdom I've asked for.

The Greater Wealth

Jesus looked at him and loved him. "One thing you lack," he said. "Go, sell everything you have and give to the poor, and you will have treasure in heaven. Then come, follow me."

At this the man's face fell. He went away sad, because he had great wealth.

—MARK 10:21-22

౭ఞ

Father, when I think of the rich man who turned away from following You because of his great wealth, it saddens me. Your Word tells me that You loved this man. And yet he obviously prized his possessions more than he valued being loved by You. What foolishness! Lord, I don't need earthly wealth in order to be content. Following close to You gives me wealth and security that this world can never know. Thank You, Lord, that I understand this. Many men do not…and they suffer dire consequences in their pursuit of earthly wealth. Lord, I do choose to follow You!

Time

Seasons of Life

There is a time for everything, and a season for every activity under heaven.

—ECCLESIASTES 3:1

❦

Thank You, Lord, for the many seasons of life. Thank You for this very season of my life I'm enjoying right now, even with the struggles involved. Help me remember that this season will endure for a short while, and then a new season—a new springtime—or winter—will come into my life.

I know this is because You are a God of forward movement, and as I find some enjoyment in this present season, I know that in the future there will be "a time for" what You have planned for me next.

Praise You, Father.

Number My Days

Teach us to number our days aright, that we may gain a heart of wisdom.

—PSALM 90:12

༄

Time is precious, Lord. I must not squander it, but rather invest it in this good life You've entrusted to me. I will see each day, Father, as a fresh and "numbered" gift from You—chock full of both opportunities and challenges. Each one will build in me a heart of wisdom as I trust You to guide me through those opportunities and provide the strength to bear the challenges I face.

The Days Are Evil

Be very careful, then, how you live—not as unwise but as wise, making the most of every opportunity, because the days are evil.

—EPHESIANS 5:15-16

∽

So much is going on in our nation right now. On one hand, the days are indeed evil...but still You give light so that we might shine in the darkness. Sometimes I'm tempted to fear the future. Will there be terrorist attacks near me? Pandemics? Financial collapse?

No matter what's ahead, I will live wisely, Lord, with Your power in me. I will make the most of every opportunity, taking care to give You praise for sustaining me in all that happens.

Life Is Short

*What is your life? You are a mist that appears for
a little while and then vanishes.*

—JAMES 4:14

∽

Every time someone I know dies, I'm reminded of
the brevity of my life. Truly I'm like a mist that appears
for only a while and then vanishes. Life *is* short. But
every Christian's life is long enough for You to accomplish Your purposes.

I don't know how long I have to live, Father, but I
do know that I have today as a gift from You. I will
treasure it as yet one more opportunity to live for You.
Thank You for my life—as brief as it is, it's still long
enough for me to find satisfaction in You.

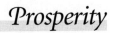

Prosperity

Diligent Hands

Lazy hands make a man poor, but diligent hands bring wealth.

—PROVERBS 10:4

❧

Lord, give me diligent hands! (And a diligent heart!) I desire to be successful in my life. I do want to prosper. I want my hands to be busy in the work You've set before me. Keep me from idleness and laziness. Work on my attitudes, Lord. Cultivate in me a spirit of achievement and godly ambition to do my best in life. Let me see the fruit of my diligence, Father. Let me see the measure of success and prosperity You mean to measure out for me.

Strong Roots

The righteous will flourish like a palm tree, they will grow like a cedar of Lebanon.

—PSALM 92:12

∞

Roots, Lord. I need good strong roots that go deep and enable me to withstand the storms. I want to flourish in all I do. Surely the motivation to succeed comes from You. I only need to trust You and move ahead, and You will prosper me as You see fit. Lord, go ahead of me and prepare the way. Remove the obstacles to success that would cause me to fail or slow down. Make my path clear, O Lord. Establish me as You would a strong cedar of Lebanon.

Thank You, Lord!

Enlarge My Territory

Jabez cried out to the God of Israel, "Oh, that you would bless me and enlarge my territory! Let your hand be with me, and keep me from harm so that I will be free from pain." And God granted his request.

—1 CHRONICLES 4:10

❧

God, as You did for Jabez, grant my request for an enlarged territory. I do cry out to You that Your hand would be with me. Keep me from harm. Expand my opportunities. Open the doors for me that I might succeed. Close the doors that are wrong for me. Make a way, Lord. Make a way for an increase in my responsibilities and gifts.

May You grant my request, Lord.

Filled to Overflowing

Honor the LORD with your wealth, with the firstfruits of
all your crops; then your barns will be filled to
overflowing, and your vats will brim over with new wine.

—PROVERBS 3:9-10

❧

All I have is Yours, Lord. Any wealth I possess is
because of Your favor...and—large or small—I thank
You for that which You have entrusted to me.

When blessings come my way, I honor You with
the firstfruits; then my barns will overflow, and my vats
will brim with new wine. I honor You with my wealth,
O Lord.

Father, You are my financial counselor and invest-
ment advisor. I pray that You would safeguard my
assets.

Hard Times

A Rough Patch

My life is consumed by anguish and my years by groaning; my strength fails because of my affliction, and my bones grow weak.

—PSALM 31:10

❧

These are hard times, Lord. People are struggling. Sometimes *I'm* struggling. My strength fails because of what's going on in my life. Help me, Lord. Give me some light at the end of my tunnel. Open doors to freedom that are now closed. Change, O God, my direction. Bring help. Bring relief. Give me Your Spirit to get me through this rough patch. Hold me up, Lord!

Increase My Strength!

*If you falter in times of trouble, how small is
your strength!*

—PROVERBS 24:10

∽

Why, O Lord, do You allow these hard times in my
life? Is it to reveal my small strength? If so, then yes,
Lord, I confess that I'm weak. But help me to have over-
coming faith, my God. Increase my ability to persevere
under this pressure. Turn my circumstances around;
even though the turn may begin slowly, let it at least
begin. Rescue me from these raging waters, O Lord. Bring
me to higher ground. Increase my faith, Lord! Soon!

I Will Rejoice

*Rejoice in the Lord always. I will say it
again: Rejoice!*

—PHILIPPIANS 4:4

∽

Sometimes, Lord, the very last thing I want to do when
stressed is rejoice. I can't see a reason for rejoicing. Life is
hard, and my focus on my circumstances drains any desire
to rejoice. And yet if my hard times persist, I have to do
something. If I can't change what's going on around me,
I have to have an inner change. Lord, if rejoicing will
change my attitude…if it will help me endure the hard
times, then I will rejoice. I will choose to rejoice in spite
of my pain over my present circumstances.

I do rejoice, Lord. I rejoice in You.

Patient in Affliction

Be joyful in hope, patient in affliction, faithful in prayer.

—ROMANS 12:12

✑

Father, Your Word instructs me to be joyful, patient, and faithful in prayer. Therefore I will rejoice in You, and I will pray. Patience may be harder, Lord. Each day is like another twenty-mile walk through the desert. When will this season of my life end, Lord? When will times of refreshing come again? I thirst for real joy, O God. I thirst for You.

Though the road ahead is obscured, I still will offer up my praise to You, Father. I pray to You. I rejoice in You. And I will be patient.

Grace

Reveling in Grace

Sin shall not be your master, because you are not under law, but under grace.

—ROMANS 6:14

Thank You, Lord, for offering grace to me. And for releasing me from the law—which I could not keep anyway. Truly, salvation is a real setting free from sin and the power of the law. When I revel in Your grace, it's like swimming freely in a vast ocean. But when I think of the law and my feeble attempts to do right, it's like struggling through a vast desert.

What joy there is in grace, Father! I glory in Your grace!

More Grace!

By the grace of God I am what I am, and his grace to me was not without effect. No, I worked harder than all of them—yet not I, but the grace of God that was with me.

—1 CORINTHIANS 15:10

✍

Sometimes, Lord, I don't *feel* Your grace at work in my life. But it is there. All the time. Your grace is making me who You have always envisioned me to be. Your grace has great effect in my life, even when I don't notice it. Your grace even has the miraculous power to change the way I relate to those around me.

Then, Lord, my prayer is: more grace to me, Lord, more grace!

Amazing Grace

In him we have redemption through his blood, the forgiveness of sins, in accordance with the riches of God's grace.

—EPHESIANS 1:7

Father God, how very rich I am! I'm a possessor of Your grace—and that makes me a wealthy man, indeed. I have redemption through Your blood. All of my many sins are forever forgiven—all because of Your amazing grace. What an incredible thought. While others still must deal with the unresolved sin in their lives, Lord, You have freed me from the guilt of all my past sins.

Lord, I praise and exalt You for the kindness You shower upon me daily. All in accordance with the riches of Your grace.

Strong in Grace

You then, my son, be strong in the grace that is in Christ Jesus.

—2 TIMOTHY 2:1

∽

Father, like most men, I like to be strong. I'd like a stronger body, a stronger sense of self-discipline…there are so many areas of my life where I want to be stronger. But, Lord, I've not often thought of grace as something in which I should be strong. But I do know that grace is powerful in my life and is the means through which I grow as a Christian man. Give me insight, Lord, on just how I can exhibit strength in grace. Help me to be a strong man in grace, so that I might extend Your grace to others.

Praise

Awesome Wonders

He is your praise; he is your God, who performed
for you those great and awesome wonders you saw
with your own eyes.

—DEUTERONOMY 10:21

∽

What wonderful things You have done for me, Lord!
I look back with awe at some of the ways You moved in
my life, even when I was unaware of it. Great and awesome wonders are Your specialty. I praise You for each
and every one. But what excites me today is to realize
that You have even more wonders planned for me in the
years to come. Even today I have the hope of unfolding
wonders in my life.

Yes, Lord, I have seen Your mighty deeds with my
own eyes, and I'm so grateful.

Glory to Your name, Father!

My Immovable Rock

The LORD lives! Praise be to my Rock! Exalted be God, the Rock, my Savior!

—2 SAMUEL 22:47

∽

Lord, I exalt You! I praise Your name! You are my Rock, my Savior, my Lord! You are unchangeable… immovable…an unceasing lover of my soul. May the very rocks cry out in praise of You and all You are. May my lips offer continual praise to You, my mighty King! I give You praise and glory. You are worthy! Hallelujah, Lord!

Night Counsel

I will praise the LORD, who counsels me; even at night my heart instructs me.

—PSALM 16:7

✍

Father, sometimes in my bed at night, before I go to sleep, I think about Your greatness. Sometimes that leads me to prayer. Sometimes in the night You counsel me. You instruct me in the way I should go. You warn me of where not to go…what not to do. You open Your Word to me. You show me great promises for my good. You show me areas of my life I need to change.

For all Your nightly counsel, I praise You. I honor You for Your commitment to me, even in the night season.

Melodies of Praise

Is any one of you in trouble? He should pray.
Is anyone happy? Let him sing songs of praise.

—JAMES 5:13

∽

Lord, to You I sing praises of thanksgiving. You have dealt mercifully and kindly with me. Your affection for me fills me with joy. Your love overwhelms me. Your joy is my constant companion. Your peace is my safeguard.

From my heart, Lord, I offer up melodies of praise and gratitude...thanksgiving for all You do and all You are.

You, my God, are my happiness.

The Holy Spirit

He Lives Within

*If you then, though you are evil, know how to give
good gifts to your children, how much more will
your Father in heaven give the Holy Spirit to those
who ask him!*

—LUKE 11:13

∽

Lord, You are a great Father to me. You give me good gifts without hesitation. You are far better than the best earthly father who has ever lived. It's hard for my mind to wrap around the paternal love You have for me. And I thank You especially, Father in heaven, for the gift of Your Holy Spirit—the best gift of all. Thank You that He lives within me and is my Comforter and the One who guides me.

Father, thank You for this unspeakable gift.

A Vessel of Love

Hope does not disappoint us, because God has poured out his love into our hearts by the Holy Spirit, whom he has given us.

—ROMANS 5:5

∽

Father, thank You for pouring out Your love into my heart. On my own, I'm not very good at loving. But by the power of Your Holy Spirit, I do love others, even those who cross me at times. Thank You, too, that this love is not feigned or manipulative but—since it originates in You—genuine. Multiply this love, Lord. Make it grow.

Your Son Forever

May the grace of the Lord Jesus Christ, and the love of God, and the fellowship of the Holy Spirit be with you all.

—2 CORINTHIANS 13:14

✍

Praise You, Father, for the grace of the Lord Jesus Christ in my life. Thank You for creating me to be Your son forever. Thank You for Your deep love toward me—a love that is really unfathomable to the human mind. And thank You, too, for my relationship with the Holy Spirit and the way He enables our good fellowship. I pray that He will continue to teach me, guide me, and comfort me.

Thank You, Lord, for this treasure called grace.

Praying in the Holy Spirit

*You, dear friends, build yourselves up in your
most holy faith and pray in the Holy Spirit.*

—JUDE 1:20

❧

Holy Spirit, teach me to pray more effectively! I want to build my faith by learning to pray with power. Give me insight, Lord, on *what* to pray for, *when* to pray, and *how* to pray. Allow my prayers to be like railroad tracks on which Your will can be the locomotive. Use my prayers, Lord, to further Your kingdom. Remind me to pray more often throughout the day, Lord—even short prayers that simply connect me with Your love.

Spirit of God, pray through me.

Thoughts

A Bold Spirit

*God did not give us a spirit of timidity, but a spirit
of love and of self-discipline.*

—2 TIMOTHY 1:7

✑

Thank You, Lord, for the boldness You give me. Not
brashness or rudeness, but the power to be straightfor-
ward about who I am and what I believe. Thank You for
the power for living right. Help me, I pray, with self-
discipline. Help me order my thoughts in a way that will
produce orderly and productive actions. A fruitful life,
Lord, is what I ask.

His Thoughts/My Thoughts

We have the mind of Christ.

—1 CORINTHIANS 2:16

❧

The ability to *think* is such a wonderful thing, Lord. And to think that my thoughts can issue from a godly mind is especially awesome. And surely "the mind of Christ" is among my greatest needs. You, Lord, know full well the contents of my natural human mind and the results of following its wandering thoughts.

But to see things through Christian eyes—that's so totally different. World events, life's circumstances, finances, relationships, and so much more—as understood by You. Help me, Father, live my life with that "mind of Christ" perspective. Teach me to humble myself as Christ humbled Himself. Give me more opportunities to serve, just as He served. May His thoughts truly be my thoughts.

Good Thinking

Brothers, whatever is true, whatever is noble,
whatever is right, whatever is pure, whatever
is lovely, whatever is admirable—if anything
is excellent or praiseworthy—think about
such things.

—PHILIPPIANS 4:8

℘

Lord, every day (sometimes every minute) it seems like my mind is assaulted with thoughts I do not choose to have. They come like darts aimed at my good intentions—and sometimes they lead me to do things I don't want to do. When these times come, Father, help me to change my thoughts to *right* things—good things that will build me up and lead to right actions.

Perfect Peace

*You will keep in perfect peace him whose mind is
steadfast, because he trusts in you.*

—ISAIAH 26:3

❧

Perfect peace is what I long for, Father. The kind of
peace that comes from keeping my mind steadfast on
You. This peace is what You promise to those who trust
in You and meditate on Your excellent ways. When something comes against me to disrupt my peace, I pray, Lord,
that You would gently guide my thoughts back to You.

Thank You, God, for perfect peace during this
present situation. Have Your hand on the circumstances,
and engineer them into an ending that is according to
Your plan.

Love

Love Is the Badge

We know that we have passed from death to life, because we love our brothers. Anyone who does not love remains in death.

—1 JOHN 3:14

✍

Love is the badge of a true Christian, and, Lord, You have given me some wonderful brothers to love. Thank You for the good friends and fellow soldiers in the faith in my life. I pray for them now…that You could increase our commitment to one another. I also pray for the opportunity to develop more friendships in the faith—more opportunities to express love to the brethren.

Thank You that I have passed from death to life… and that my love for my brothers in Christ is the proof.

Love: My Binding Force

*Let love and faithfulness never leave you; bind
them around your neck, write them on the tablet
of your heart.*

—PROVERBS 3:3

∽

I choose, Lord, to be a man who loves. I bind love
and faithfulness around my neck, so to speak. I cleave
to love as a guiding force in my life. Show me ways to
demonstrate love and concern to those I meet. Provide
divine opportunities for me to be a giver to, rather than
a taker from, those I know. Bind me together with those
who know Your love. May we be one in Christ.

One Divine Quality

Now these three remain: faith, hope and love.
But the greatest of these is love.

—1 CORINTHIANS 13:13

∽

Love triumphs over all else. Love is the greatest gift. Even though I have faith and hope, help me remember that love is even better, for out of love flows all else: forgiveness, patience, good works—all that I must be as a Christian springs from this one divine quality: love. May it be mine in abundance, Father.

My Christian Brothers

*We always thank God, the Father of our Lord
Jesus Christ, when we pray for you, because we
have heard of your faith in Christ Jesus and of the
love you have for all the saints.*

—COLOSSIANS 1:3-4

∽

There are Christian brothers in foreign lands who
are suffering because of their faith in You, Lord. I will
not forget them. I pray Your blessing on them, Father,
for their enduring faith. Remind me daily to lift them up
in prayer. Also, please send provision to the many Christians around the world who are hungry and without
hope. Send workers. Send *me*, if necessary. But certainly
hear my prayers for them. Bless them, Lord, and show
me my part in easing their suffering.

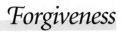 *Forgiveness*

Seventy Times Seven

Peter came to Jesus and asked,

"Lord, how many times shall I forgive my brother when he sins against me? Up to seven times?"

Jesus answered, "I tell you, not seven times, but seventy-seven times."

—MATTHEW 18:21-22

∽

Endless forgiveness, Lord. That's what You want from me. But sometimes forgiveness is hard. Not just for me… but no doubt also for those whom I've wronged. I do need their forgiveness, Lord…and I need Your forgiveness too. Help me to be a great forgiver, just as You are the great forgiver of all my sins. Help me keep short accounts on those who have wronged me. May I learn to forgive trespasses instantly, just as You forgive mine.

All on Account of Christ

I write to you, dear children, because your sins
have been forgiven on account of his name.

—1 JOHN 2:12

∽

   Forgiveness of sin is such a great blessing, Lord. It's hard for me to fathom the depth of Your forgiveness toward me. You have forgiven it all. Yes, *all* of it. Every sin has been laid on Christ, charged to Him.

   Lord, I have to stop for a moment when I think of it. And then I must praise You for this incredible undeserved mercy. All on account of Christ. Praise You, Lord. It still baffles me that You love me so much.

A Blessed Man

*Blessed is he whose transgressions are forgiven,
whose sins are covered. Blessed is the man whose
sin the LORD does not count against him and in
whose spirit is no deceit.*

—PSALM 32:1-2

∽

I am a blessed man, Lord. *Blessed!* My past sins are all covered…gone forever. And You do not count sin against me. What a display of love toward me! Father, thank You for this zero balance in my sin account. Not only that, but I have an infinite positive balance in my grace account. Your riches of forgiveness and grace toward me make me not only blessed, but incredibly wealthy. Thank You, Father!

Total Forgiveness

Bear with each other and forgive whatever
grievances you may have against one another.
Forgive as the Lord forgave you.

—COLOSSIANS 3:13

❧

God, if there is anyone from whom I'm withholding forgiveness, please reveal that person to me. I do want to be forgiving toward all who have offended me. I want to replicate in my small human way Your forgiveness toward me. And that Your forgiveness was *total* forgiveness.

Father, each day I pray that You will immediately uncover any unresolved situations that require me to forgive or be forgiven.

The Poor

God Remembers

Cornelius answered: "Four days ago I was in my house praying at this hour, at three in the afternoon. Suddenly a man in shining clothes stood before me and said, 'Cornelius, God has heard your prayer and remembered your gifts to the poor.'"

—ACTS 10:30-31

༕

God, You hear our prayers, and You remember our gifts to the poor. What a revelation. Though You forgive and forget our sins, You *remember* our gifts to the poor. The poor must therefore always be on Your mind, Father. May they, then, always be on my mind too. Increase my sensitivity, Lord, to the poor around me. Open my eyes to see the need and to see what You'd have me do. Use me, Lord, to remember these ones who are always on Your mind.

Rolling Up My Sleeves

*All they asked was that we should continue to
remember the poor, the very thing I was eager to do.*

—GALATIANS 2:10

∽

Father, may I, like the apostle Paul, be *eager* to
remember the poor. It's such an easy thing, really. And
You have entrusted me with so much in comparison to
the poor around me. Help me understand, Lord, when
and how to share what You've given me. And show me,
too, how I can roll up my sleeves and put my concerns
into action. Lord, lift the burden of the poor…and use
me to help.

Open My Ears, Lord

They caused the cry of the poor to come before him, so that he heard the cry of the needy.

—JOB 34:28

∽

Thank You, Lord, for hearing the cry of the needy. Their prayers are before You night and day. Even now as I pray, others in greater need than I am are also praying. Lord, hear our prayers. Meet our needs—whether financial, spiritual, or emotional—in abundance.

As You open Your ears to the cry of the poor, open mine as well. Let me not just be a hearer of Your Word, but also a doer…especially as it relates to the poor. Lord, I cry out to You on behalf of the needy.

Jesus in Disguise

The righteous will answer him, "Lord, when did we see you hungry and feed you, or thirsty and give you something to drink? When did we see you a stranger and invite you in, or needing clothes and clothe you? When did we see you sick or in prison and go to visit you?" The King will reply, "I tell you the truth, whatever you did for one of the least of these brothers of mine, you did for me."

—MATTHEW 25:37-40

∽

Lord, You come to us today in disguise. We can see You in the poor and the hungry; the stranger and the prisoner. You are dwelling today among the least of the brothers...the last place most people would expect to find You.

Father, I want to find You there. I hear Your words of warning and I respond by offering myself for Your use. I desire to see You fed, given drink, invited in, clothed, made well, and visited. Show me, then, how to minister to Your needs among those in need. I will follow.

Pride

Never Forget!

*Be careful that you do not forget the L*ORD* your God, failing to observe his commands, his laws and his decrees that I am giving you this day. Otherwise, when you eat and are satisfied, when you build fine houses and settle down, and when your herds and flocks grow large and your silver and gold increase and all you have is multiplied, then your heart will become proud and you will forget the L*ORD* your God, who brought you out of Egypt, out of the land of slavery.*

—ĐEUTERONOMY 8:11-14

∽

Lord, may I never forget! Lord, keep it ever before me that all I have and all I am is because YOU sought me, saved me, and prospered me. How can I, then, ever find a reason to be prideful? The truth is, there is *no* reason why I can boast for anything in my life.

I will never forget, Father, all that You've done for me. I praise You for the days ahead. Surely blessings are around the corner. You have not finished with me yet, Lord!

Avoiding a Downfall

Before his downfall a man's heart is proud,
but humility comes before honor.

—PROVERBS 18:12

∽

Knowing that an ultimate downfall awaits the prideful keeps me humble, Lord! What foolishness to think that man should boast of his own achievements and possessions. Lord, You are the giver of all good things. And, with me, You have found effective ways to keep me humble. May it ever be so, Lord. I do not aspire to a proud heart but take comfort in my lowly estate. Lowliness has the greater blessings!

Living in Harmony

*Live in harmony with one another. Do not be
proud, but be willing to associate with people of
low position. Do not be conceited.*

—ROMANS 12:16

✍

Lord, You give and You take away. I take note of
Your call to humility. I abhor conceit and the prideful-
ness that so easily rears its head. Yes, Lord, sometimes
I'm tempted to think more of myself than I ought. Guard
me from such false pretense.

Do not let me choose my friends based on how they
can help advance me. Rather, help me choose friends to
whom I can be of help. I do not look on the outward
appearance, Lord, but I try to see what's inside a person:
honor, integrity, and potential.

Lord, Let Me Love

*Love is patient, love is kind. It does not envy, it
does not boast, it is not proud.*

—1 CORINTHIANS 13:4

❧

Lord, a lover of God must not be full of pride. From
time to time You have given me glimpses of why there's
really no room in my life for pride. You call to mind the
times I trusted in myself and failed. Or the times I said
something that hurt another person. The times I've tried
to maneuver something I wanted to happen and felt
needed my "help." Those are among the most painful
memories, Father.

Lord, let me simply love. Let me be free of all the
prideful hindrances to love.

Open my heart, Lord.

Helping Others

Giving a Blessing

Do to others as you would have them do to you.

—LUKE 6:31

༄

This life really isn't about me, is it, Lord? It's about You. But while I'm in this human body, it's also about others and how I can help them achieve their goals. God, You know how helpful others have been in my life. They were surely Your messengers to keep me on the right road. Now, Father, allow me to do for others, what others have done for me. Let me sow seeds where I have already harvested a good crop.

Show me, today, how I can be a blessing to someone else.

Selfish Ambitions

Do nothing out of selfish ambition or vain conceit, but in humility consider others better than yourselves.

—PHILIPPIANS 2:3

✍

Sometimes, Father, my ambitions get the best of me. This life You gave me has so much potential. But, Lord, I know that if I put aside my selfish ambitions and look to the needs of others, You will bless me. Even open doors for me. There are so many good traits I personally lack that I notice in others. In that way, it's easy to consider others better than myself. Perhaps, then, others can see something in me that's good. If so, You and I both know that's simply the work You've done in my life.

Thank You, Lord, for the silent, under-the-radar work that You do in my life.

Solid Relationships

Be devoted to one another in brotherly love.
Honor one another above yourselves.

—ROMANS 12:10

❧

Seeing Jesus in others can be easy...or hard. Some brothers are hard to love, hard to even get to know well. Sometimes it seems like there's a wall that must be penetrated before I can know them. Lord, keep me from having such a wall around me. And give me the patience to keep trying to build solid relationships with other good brothers. Give me men in my life I can honor above myself.

Bind Us Together, Lord

How good and pleasant it is when brothers live together in unity!

—PSALM 133:1

⁓

Your will is that Your people be one, Lord. That they be united. Sometimes that's not so easy. But, God, I want the peaceable life that comes from dwelling in unity with others. I pray You would put an end to potential or existing strife that would disrupt the unity I have with the Christian brothers I know. Help me sow the seeds that will yield the fruit of unity among us. May we learn to allow Your love to be the glue that binds us together. For Your church worldwide, Lord, I pray for unity in the midst of a turbulent and rebellious world. Bind us together, Lord.

The Words of My Mouth

Guard My Mouth

*Set a guard over my mouth, O Lord; keep watch
over the door of my lips.*

—PSALM 141:3

∽

Sometimes, Lord, I speak without thinking. I say
things I immediately wish I could take back. Sometimes
it's to a friend, a coworker, or, worse, to members of my
own family. I've hurt these people by my quick mouth.

Lord, even as I ask for their forgiveness, I also ask
for You to guard my mouth. Keep watch over my lips.
Give me pause when I think I'm ready to speak. Let me
ask myself if my words are edifying or destructive. If the
latter, help me to swallow them quickly before they
escape my mouth.

Lord, guard my lips!

About My Fuse, Lord

My dear brothers, take note of this: Everyone
should be quick to listen, slow to speak and slow to
become angry.

—JAMES 1:19

∽

Like many men, Lord, sometimes my fuse is short.
Too short. I get angry at a person or situation, and before
I know it, I've spewed my anger all over anyone within
earshot. That ought not to be, and I know it. I'm just too
quick to react in those situations.

Calm me down, Lord. Remove my fuse. Remind me to
listen before I speak. I mean really *listen*. May I hear through
ready ears and speak with a not-so-ready mouth.

Heart Surgery

Out of the overflow of the heart the mouth speaks.

—MATTHEW 12:34

❧

Lord, where do my words come from? Your Word says they come out of my heart. Sometimes that's a disturbing thought. But that being the case, Lord, I need some heart surgery.

I pray that You would remove the negativity from my heart and allow it to overflow with an attitude that will spill forth in *good* words for those to whom I speak.

Yes, Lord, give me the heart of a man who speaks wisdom and love.

Give me Your heart, O Lord.

A Good Man

The mouth of the righteous man utters wisdom,
and his tongue speaks what is just.

—PSALM 37:30

৵

Lord, I would like to be known by others as a good man. Not prideful, but good nonetheless. And surely both my deeds and my words will be how I'm judged on that score. So, Lord, You know that in myself I'm not as wise as I should be. My tongue certainly bears that out at times. Instruct me, God, in wisdom. Alert my eyes to situations where You have something to teach me. And as I learn, may I speak to others what is just and right in Your sight. A good word in due season, Lord. That's how I'd like to speak.

Confidence

The Source of My Confidence

As for me, I watch in hope for the LORD, I wait for God my Savior; my God will hear me.

—MICAH 7:7

∽

You, O Lord, are my confidence! When I pray, You hear me and answer. Praise be to Your Name for the confidence You give me. Who can come against me when I belong to You, O Lord? No one! I take refuge in You. I find my strength in You. All my hopes are wrapped up in YOU, O Lord.

May my days be blessed because I have made You the source of my confidence, O God.

A Mighty Warrior

The LORD is with me like a mighty warrior; so my persecutors will stumble and not prevail. They will fail and be thoroughly disgraced; their dishonor will never be forgotten.

—JEREMIAH 20:11

❦

Some men perceive of You as weak, if they perceive You at all, Lord. And yet You are strong! You are a mighty warrior! A mighty warrior on my behalf! Those who would unfairly persecute me or try to make me fail will answer to You. Thank You for protecting my name, Lord. For taking up my cause. Thank You for Your excellent strength. You are *my* mighty warrior!

Keep My Foot, O Lord

*The LORD will be your confidence and will keep
your foot from being snared.*

—PROVERBS 3:26

❧

All those many times, Lord, that I seem to stumble,
I forget that You are my confidence. Why do I keep on
trusting in myself or in others for my future? What a
waste of time. You are in charge of my steps. You direct
my paths. You, O God, keep my foot from the snares
that would trap me. My Father, You are my extreme
confidence. In You alone will I boldly trust!

The God Who Sees Ahead

The fruit of righteousness will be peace; the effect of righteousness will be quietness and confidence forever.

—ISAIAH 32:17

༄

There are so many benefits to serving You, Lord. Surely one of the best is the peace that I have: the quiet confidence that nothing can rattle. I have only to remind myself that You are my Lord 24/7 and nothing regarding me can happen without first passing through Your hands.

O God, I do not worry about the future; I have Your quiet unshakeable confidence. Thank You for seeing the dangerous things ahead that I cannot yet see. Thank You for going ahead of me and clearing the way through the underbrush, so that as I pass through the dry lands, I come out the other side unscathed.

Praise You, God, for Your abounding love toward me!

Desires

A Good Heritage

The desire of the righteous ends only in good, but the hope of the wicked only in wrath.

—PROVERBS 11:23

༂

Father, You cause all things to work together for my good. Even my desires will end in good for me. What a heritage I have! When I contrast that with the complete loss that those who turn away from You must endure, it takes my breath away. How then could any reasonable person say no to You?

Lord, please know that I say yes to You and Your will. Both today and forever.

Fill My Heart, Lord

*May the LORD answer you when you are in
distress; may the name of the God of Jacob protect
you…May he give you the desire of your heart
and make all your plans succeed.*

—PSALM 20:1,4

Lord, sometimes I wonder about my "plans." I confess
that sometimes I plan…and then almost as an afterthought,
I ask You to bless those plans. That's not good. Instead,
Father, I pray that the desires of my heart and the resulting
plans I make would find their source in You.

I pray then, Lord, for You to fill my heart with the
right desires that will satisfy Your plan and give me an
assurance of being used by You.

A Clear Conscience

*Pray for us. We are sure that we have a clear
conscience and desire to live honorably in every way.*

—HEBREWS 13:18

♋

Lord, how satisfying when, with a clear conscience, I can desire only to live in such a way as to honor You in all I do. I pray, Lord, for a clear mind and firm resolve to accomplish Your vision for my life. I pray for opportunities to live honorably in every circumstance...even when doing so might cause me loss. Father, Your blessing follows those who have their desires rooted in doing Your will—and I desire those blessings following behind me.

Bold in Prayer

I tell you, whatever you ask for in prayer, believe that you have received it, and it will be yours.

—MARK 11:24

∽

The highest privilege of a Christian man is surely having the power of prayer. Thank You, Lord, that You instituted this wonderful way of fellowshipping with You. You actually ask us to come to You boldly with our requests. And even though You know my every need before I even utter it, You still bid me to pray. And so I do pray. Daily, I ask You for the things that I need to be the man You called me to be. Lord, as I pray, I do believe. Thank You for the unbreakable promise that You hear and answer my prayers.